AF575921

NAVAL

Sōryū, Hiryū, & Unryū-Class Aircraft Carriers

In the Imperial Japanese Navy during World War II

LARS AHLBERG & HANS LENGERER

Library of Congress Control Number: 2020930939

Designed by Justin Watkinson
Type set in Impact/Minion Pro/Univers LT Std

ISBN: 978-0-7643-6077-0
Printed in China

Published by Schiffer Publishing, Ltd.
4880 Lower Valley Road
Atglen, PA 19310
Phone: (610) 593-1777; Fax: (610) 593-2002
E-mail: Info@schifferbooks.com
www.schifferbooks.com

For our complete selection of fine books on this and related subjects, please visit our website at www.schifferbooks.com. You may also write for a free catalog.

Schiffer Publishing's titles are available at special discounts for bulk purchases for sales promotions or premiums. Special editions, including personalized covers, corporate imprints, and excerpts, can be created in large quantities for special needs. For more information, contact the publisher.

We are always looking for people to write books on new and related subjects. If you have an idea for a book, please contact us at proposals@schifferbooks.com.

Acknowledgments

In compiling this brief history of the medium-sized Japanese aircraft carriers, we are indebted to the following individuals who for a long time have given invaluable help in our research of the Imperial Japanese Navy: Messrs. Endō Akira, Fujita Takashi, Hayashi Yoshikazu, Ishibashi Takao, Itani Jirō, Iwasaki Yutaka, Izumi Kōzō, Kamakura Takumi, Kimata Jirō, Kitagawa Ken'ichi, Kitamura Kunio, Koike Naohiko, Kuroyama Kazuo, Maejima Hajime, Mizutani Kiyotaka, Morino Tetsuo, Naitō Hatsuho (via Itani), Nakagawa Tsutomu, Takagi Hiroshi, Takahashi Shigeo, Takasu Kōichi, Tamura Toshio, Todaka Kazushige, Tsuda Fumio, and Tsukamoto Hideki.

Special thanks go to Messrs. Dan Kaplan and Eugen Pinak for supplying additional photos and to Messrs. Manfred Pasch, Jürg Tischhauser, Waldemar Trojca, and Michael Wünschmann for drawings. Photos and drawings are from Hans Lengerer's *Technical and Operational History of the Aircraft Carriers of the IJN and IJA* (Katowice: Model Hobby, 2019, ISBN 978-3-86619-154-9).

All photos are from the authors' collections unless otherwise noted.

Contents

CHAPTER 1
Background

Introduction

The Imperial Japanese Navy (IJN) planned the construction of a total of forty-five aircraft carriers (CVs) in the warship-building programs from 1918 to 1942 and commissioned twenty-five of them in the twenty-year period from 1922 to 1944. These types were large, medium, and small (attack) aircraft carriers (CVAs and CVLs), some converted from other warship classes, and escort aircraft carriers (CVEs) remodeled from passenger ships. Among the CVAs the medium type formed the majority, with a total of eighteen planned. Five were completed, three remained in various completion stages at the end of the Pacific War, and ten had to be canceled.

In contrast to the impression the total number may impart, the building of the medium type was not favored because of the IJN's belief that this type represented the most suited one, but because of the lack of materiel and labor force and the insufficient production capacity during the Pacific War.

After two small and two large aircraft carriers were completed, which have to be regarded as trial ships before the execution of several modification conversions, the medium type emerged from the complete revision of the designs of the flying-deck cruisers, on the basis of the stipulations of the London Arms Limitation Treaty (1930). The design of the first representative of this class—*Sōryū*—suffered somewhat from a too-progressive procedure, indicating partial defects in the full understanding and application of fundamental laws in ship construction. This defect was eradicated in the quasi sister—the larger *Hiryū*. With her design, the IJN established the general specifications and arrangement of all future carriers, except for the position of the bridge structure, which was to port instead of starboard.

The Washington Arms Limitation Treaty ended at the end of 1936. Without being tied by qualitative and quantitative restrictions, the IJN changed its aircraft carrier–building policy: first to a remarkably enlarged version of the medium type, with greatly improved offensive and defensive power (Shōkaku class), and subsequently to a type eliminating the "defects" of the previous class and also armoring the flight deck (*Taihō*).

However, irrespective of the opinion of the strategists that this type of large attack aircraft carrier would best respond to the kind of warfare devised against its principal hypothetical enemy, the dramatic worsening of relations between Japan and the United States forced the IJN, in view of its production capacity and other factors, to return to the medium type in the last prewar building planning, because this type was easier, quicker, and cheaper to produce.

It was by the foregoing that the IJN selected this type for mass (series) production immediately after the catastrophic loss of the sisters *Sōryū* and *Hiryū* and the much-larger *Akagi* and *Kaga* (converted from a battle cruiser and a battleship, respectively, of the famous Eight-Eight Fleet) in the Battle of Midway in June 1942.

Fifteen ships of a slightly simplified *Hiryū* type (with the bridge structure located as in *Sōryū*) were to be built as the Unryū and the modified Unryū classes and to be completed from 1944 to 1947. This planning ended with two complete and three incomplete ships and confirmed the truth of the saying (at least for an inferior country) that ships have to be built before the outbreak of a war and not after.

The Sōryū, Hiryū, and Unryū classes are dealt with in common, and some details on construction aspects are given because *Hiryū*'s design and construction drawings were also used for the Unryū class, with some important revisions, the most important being the location of the island bridge. These ships were almost sisters, and they also formed the majority of the aircraft carriers originally designed as such. The Urgent Carrier Reinforcement Program, which permitted the building of the Unryū class, is briefly mentioned.

Judging from the statement that most of the aircraft carriers designed as such belonged to the medium-sized type, one might assume that the IJN preferred this type and considered it the representative and, perhaps, most "economical" aircraft carrier type. However, is this conclusion right, and did the IJN really lay chief importance upon the medium-sized carriers? Why should the IJN, always striving for maximum fighting power by individual superiority, thrust this principle aside and apparently be satisfied with a medium type, capable of providing average but not superior fighting power? Was this type not the result of the restrictions of the Washington and London Arms Limitation systems rather than a type considered by the IJN's tacticians and strategists to achieve the requirements best (i.e., the role assigned to the carrier in the strategic conception)? If this type was considered to be sufficient, why did the IJN immediately after the termination of the arms limitation system switch to the bigger Shōkaku class,[1] with superior offensive and defensive capabilities, and later expand the latter property to almost maximum in the subsequent *Taihō*? And why were two modified Taihō-class carriers and one medium-type carrier included in the Fifth Naval Armament Replenishment Program (a program that had to be totally revised after the Battle of Midway)? Why should the medium type be built not depending upon *Hiryū* but a new design? Was the change to the medium-sized type and the requirement for simplification in the Wartime Warship Urgent Building Program immediately before the beginning of the hostilities not an expression of insufficient building capacity and industrial power, rather than the belief in the advantages of this type? And was this recognition not also the decisive factor for focusing on this type in the Modified Fifth Naval Armament Replenishment Program after the defeat in the Battle of Midway? Was the characterization of the medium type as an "almost ideal" carrier and even an "ideal" carrier by Japanese authors no exaggeration to conceal imperfect properties and disguise the true conditions? And did the IJN really not want to infringe treaty regulations by the limitation of the tonnage and postponement of the building of the second carrier (later *Hiryū*) until *Hōshō* became overage and could be replaced, according to the regulations? These questions cannot be answered simply by "yes" or "no" but require the investigation of strategic and technical matters.

Political Dimensions

The London Treaty[2]

After the change of governments in the United States (Herbert Hoover elected president on March 4, 1929) and Britain (Ramsay MacDonald elected prime minister on June 7, 1929), both countries approached each other in the "cruiser question" and came to an agreement when the British premier visited the United States in October 1929.

The invitation of the British Foreign Ministry was accepted by all signatory powers of the Washington Treaty. The deliberations began on January 21, 1930, and ended on April 22 with the signing of the London Treaty.[3]

As for the aircraft carrier, the treaty did not change the total tonnage but defined the carrier in article 3, no. 1. It was completely new and replaced the definition in chapter II, part 4, of the Washington Treaty and said that every surface warship, irrespective of its displacement, that was "designed for the specific and exclusive purpose of carrying aircraft and so constructed that aircraft can be launched therefrom and landed thereon" was an aircraft carrier. Further regulations were contained in articles 4 and 5 with regard to tonnage and maximum gun caliber (155 mm).

The immediate consequence for the carrier was that *Hōshō* lost her character as an experimental carrier and had to be added to the total tonnage, as had the less-than-10,000-ton *Ryūjō*.[4] The official standard displacement of the Japanese carriers increased to 68,370 tons (*Hōshō*, 7,470 tons; *Akagi* and *Kaga*, 26,900 tons each; *Ryūjō*, 7,100 tons). Therefore, only 12,630 tons were at the disposal. The gunnery armament of a newly built carrier was limited to 155 mm because article 4 had to be applied.

The Planning of an Aircraft Carrier in the First Naval Armament Replenishment Program of 1931

After the conclusion of the London Treaty, the IJN not only pressed upon the maximum power of the ships whose tonnage had been restricted, but also wanted more units of the not-restricted classes. In addition, the naval air force, which was not limited, was also to be increased.

On June 27, 1930, Navy Minister Adm. Takarabe Takeshi received from the chief of Naval General Staff, Adm. Taniguchi Naomi, the draft of a building program with basic recommendations for the replenishment of the navy after the London Treaty. Among the 117 ships, twenty-eight air groups, and several improvement programs (in total ¥733,633,557) was also one carrier of 9,850-ton standard displacement, whose construction would begin immediately after the passing of the building program in the Diet. After drastic reductions to thirty-nine ships and approximately ¥374,000,000, the program passed the 59th session of the Diet (December 26, 1930–March 28, 1931); the carrier had become a victim of the "red pencil."[5]

The General Arms Limitation Conference of the League of Nations in 1932

The American and British proposals, which aimed for the reduction of the total tonnage by keeping the ratio decided by the Washington Treaty, were rejected by Japan. On December 9, 1932, Ambassador Matsudaira Tsuneo and Adm. Nagano Osami presented the Japanese proposal containing qualitative and quantitative limitations. The goal was the abolishment of the 5:5:3 ratios and the reduction of the range of heavy cruisers due to the reduction of the displacement. Carriers were to be abolished completely, and on the decks of warships or other ships, no installations for takeoff and landing of planes were to be permitted. In company with the aircraft carrier, attack planes were to be abolished. The intention was again obvious: the United States should be deprived of the weapon that endangered Japan most, irrespective of its favorable geopolitical situation. Before the Japanese proposals could be dealt with finally, however, the Japanese delegation left the conference on January 24, 1933, and, on March 27, the League of Nations also left due to the findings in the Lytton Report.

The Design of a Flying-Deck Cruiser

The London Treaty not only included quantitative limitation of the cruiser tonnage and the number of ships (for Japan, twelve heavy cruisers of 108,400 tons and 100,450 tons of light cruisers) but also regulated, in article 16, no. 5, that "not more than twenty-five percent of the allowed total in the cruiser category may by fitted with a landing-on platform or deck of aircraft." Article 3, no. 2, stated that "The fitting of a landing-on or flying-off platform or deck on a capital ship, cruiser or destroyer . . . shall not cause any vessel so fitted to be charged against or classified in the category of aircraft carriers."

By this definition, the rumor that flying-deck cruisers (*kōkūjunyōkan*) would be built in the United States was no more recognized as just a rumor but as a real danger. Against this background, the proposal for the abolishment of aircraft carriers and the prohibition of aviation installations on the decks of ships at the previously mentioned League of Nations Conference must be recognized. In order to oppose these ships, a flying-deck cruiser was designed by the Navy Technical Department in 1932, as basic design number (*kihon keikaku bangō*) G 6. However, the character of this ship was rather more like an aircraft carrier than a flying-deck cruiser.

The official trial displacement of the 240-meter-long design was to be 17,500 tons. On the fo'c'sle (forecastle) deck, three 20.3 cm twin-turret model E (elevation angle 70°) were arranged, pyramid-like. Immediately aft of them, the 194.2-meter-long flying deck (truly a flight deck) began and ended with a projection over the stern. A total of seventy fighters and torpedo bombers (reserve planes included) were to be carried. The high-angle guns were six type 89, 40-caliber, 12.7 cm twin mounts. The large island bridge to starboard and the funnel arrangement (also to starboard, projecting out of the hull at about half the height of the freeboard and bent aft) were remarkable features, as was the high speed of 36 knots, which was to be attained with engines generating 150,000 shaft horsepower (shp).

However, the rumor proved to be unfounded, and this design was abolished before being included in a building program. Without doubt, this ship would have become top heavy with insufficient stability and might also have suffered from lack of strength, considering the then-existing tendency during a very progressive period.

CHAPTER 2

The Building of *Sōryū* and *Hiryū*

The Second Naval Armament Replenishment Program of 1934

Japanese foreign relations were in tension since the outbreak of the Manchurian Incident and gradually worsened after leaving the League of Nations. In view of future arms limitation conferences and the tendency of Japan's isolation, which became apparent, the highest military authorities were under the impression that the safety of the whole of East Asia depended on Japan's actual power. The Japanese-American conflict about the Manchurian question was far from being solved. The concentration of the US Fleet on the Pacific coast, the proposal of representative Carl Vinson to expand the United States Navy (USN) within the border of both arms limitation treaties (January 4, 1932), and President Franklin D. Roosevelt's Executive Order 6174 (two aircraft carriers, nine cruisers, twenty destroyers, four submarines, two gunboats) were recognized in Japan as indications of an "armed solution" of the Manchurian question, requiring urgent replenishment of the naval force.

Prince Fushimi Hiroyasu, who had relieved Adm. Taniguchi Naomi as chief of the Naval General Staff on February 2, 1932, proposed countermeasures to Navy Minister Ōsami Mineo (Naval General Staff Secret Document No. 154, dated May 6, 1933). With reference to the international situation and in addition to the replenishment of the naval air force and the warships during and after fiscal year 1934, the numerical inferiority was to be compensated for by improved quality[1] in order to attain a national defense level that permitted the Japanese to overcome the crisis. Details were to be worked out by the vice chief of the Naval General Staff and the vice navy minister.

Irrespective of this general guideline, the principle of "quantity before quality" was to be valid for carriers, because of their vulnerability to attacks, and parity, at least, should be kept with the USN. This principle took into consideration not only the maintenance of the inferiority ratio in the London Treaty vis-à-vis the USN and Royal Navy (RN), but also the result of a study according to which Japan was not able to meet concurrence with these naval powers as for naval armament.

The IJN had four (*Hōshō*, *Akagi*, *Kaga*, *Ryūjō*) carriers, and the USN had three (*Saratoga*, *Lexington*, *Ranger*). The operational value of *Hōshō*—the pioneer of this category—was limited, the *Ryūjō* was a failure, and *Akagi* and *Kaga*, before conversion, were not more than experimental carriers. In contrast, the carriers of the USN possessed all properties of modern, powerful ships. To make matters worse, Executive Order 6174 permitted the construction of two more aircraft carriers (later *Yorktown* and *Enterprise*). The carrier that had been included in the First Naval Armament Replenishment Program of 1931 had been stricken for financial reasons, but behind this official reason, one might suppose the fact that carriers of less than 10,000 tons were now to be included in the total tonnage, while, on the other hand, the fighting power was low.[2] In view of the strengthening of the USN and the tense relation with this country, the IJN deemed it absolutely necessary to use the permitted total tonnage and to build two medium-sized carriers. The "free tonnage" of 12,630 tons could be increased to 20,100 tons by the decommissioning of *Hōshō* according to article VIII of the Washington Treaty, because article 9 of the London Treaty referred to this paragraph for replacement of aircraft carriers. In order not to infringe the treaty stipulations, the displacement of each vessel was restricted to 10,050 tons. In addition, the second ship could not to be completed before 1938, the date that *Hōshō* could be deleted and replaced.

On June 14, 1933, the navy minister received the proposal as Naval General Staff Secret Document No. 199, dated June 12. Eighty-six warships displacing 159,370 tons were to be built. For the two aircraft carriers, controlled by treaty stipulations (as were twenty more ships), the Naval General Staff required the following characteristics:

Standard displacement	10,050 tons
Armament	five 20 cm low-angle guns mounted on the centerline 20 12.7 cm high-angle guns >40 machine guns
Aircraft	approx. 100
Speed	36 knots
Range	18 knots / 10,000 miles

Notes:

1. Diesel engines should, if possible, be used as propulsion system.
2. More than half the number of planes should be carried on the flight deck – ready for take-off. Aviation facilities should be planned for speedy take-off and landing procedures, as well as fast and easy operation of the aircraft carrier. If necessary, the number of reserve planes should be reduced in order to attain the goals.

In company with these two carriers, the Naval General Staff also required the construction of two fast tankers (AOs) and three seaplane carriers (AVs), with the intention to, if necessary (that is, an armed conflict or war), convert them into light aircraft carriers (CVLs), because it was believed that parity with the USN could not be attained when the USN was expanded. With this program, which passed the 65th Diet session (December 28, 1933–March 26, 1934) in reduced form (forty-eight ships of 137,350 tons) and became law on March 20, 1934, after Imperial sanction, the IJN began its policy of "concealed ships." This is the background to why the Second Naval Armament Replenishment Program of 1934 was known by the few intimate as the "Latent Aircraft Carrier Construction Program" (*Sensaiteki Kōkūbokan no Kenzō*).

Revision of the Requirements and Original Design of the *Sōryū*

Design G 6 had a standard displacement of about 12,000 tons. The basis for this design was fewer aircraft, fewer high-angle guns, no machine guns, a shorter flight deck (and hangars), and only one 20.3 cm gun more than the new requirement. With only one gun less but more requirements in all other characteristics, it was quite obvious that the "wishes" of the Naval General Staff could not be fulfilled within the tonnage restriction. In order to avoid the defects of such ships as *Ryūjō*, 22,000–25,000 tons would have been necessary.[3] Unfortunately, the authors cannot provide a logical explanation, but some Japanese authors suppose that the requirement was made after consultations with the Navy Technical Department (this was the usual procedure), and that the standard displacement should conceal only the true character of the ship.[4] However, maybe because of resistance from the Navy Technical Department or because of their own realizations, the Navy Technical Department received new requirements early in 1933:

Standard displacement	10,050 tons (peacetime), 11,000 tons (wartime)
Main guns	5 15.5 cm low-angle guns (one triple, one twin turret)
High-angle guns	8 12.7 cm twin mounts
Machine-guns	approx. 40
Aircraft	approx. 70
Range	18 knots / 10,000 miles

The design executed as basic design no. G 8 was completed in the autumn of 1933 and was later called the original design of *Sōryū*. It had some features, particularly the far-projecting flight deck at the stern, similar to the later Royal Navy carrier *Ark Royal*, and the large island bridge to starboard was positioned about one-third of the length from the bow, with the staircase-like shape at the front side and concentrated fire control systems and rangefinders. Something new was the vertical funnel arranged aft of the island bridge.[5] The two turrets, with 15.5 cm low-angle guns, were to be situated on the fo'c'sle (anchor deck) beneath the flight deck.[6] The number of 12.7 cm high-angle guns was reduced to twelve from sixteen, and these were to be placed on sponsons, with comparatively good arcs of fire, in the aft half of the hull.

As a carrier design, G 8 was remarkably better than G 6; as an artillery ship, it was much inferior. To make matters still worse, armor protection—of G 6 comparable to the heavy cruisers of the Myōkō class—of G 8 was never adequate for a gunnery duel. The protection of the ammunition magazines was to be against 20 cm projectiles; the other vital parts were to be protected against 12.7 cm shells. The intended mounting of low-angle guns can hardly be understood, because the IJN knew perfectly well that no carrier was suited for this; instead it had weapons capable of attacking, damaging, and sinking any ship within the range of its aircraft—far outside the range of guns. That carriers had to be protected by antisubmarine warfare and antiaircraft vessels against submarine and aircraft attacks, and also against artillery ships, was commonly known, and the operations of aircraft carriers as part of a force composed of such ships had been discussed in numerous publications. It could have been that tacticians in the Naval General Staff were so impressed by the rumor of American flying-deck cruisers that a counterpart should be created. If so, the blunder of the 20 cm low-angle gun armament of *Akagi* and *Kaga* during the aftermath of the Washington Treaty would have been repeated under the much-tenser situation following the London Treaty. The requirement of mounting low-angle guns automatically added a considerable amount of equipment weight not necessary in a carrier. In view of the quantitative inferiority in carrier tonnage and the recognition that, at least, a numerical parity with the USN should be kept, improvement of carrier features and not a hybrid with limited proficiency for either purpose should have been aimed for.

Like other ships designed in that period, the excessive requirements of the Naval General Staff were reflected in the final designs, and the basic design had features that simply could not have been incorporated within the given tonnage.

At the end of 1933—that is, even before the passing of the building program by the Diet—Kure Navy Yard secretly received the building order for the first ship, and early in 1934, preparations for construction and the production of armor plates began.

Effect of the Capsizing of the Torpedo Boat *Tomozuru* and Revision of the Design

When the torpedo boat *Tomozuru* capsized on March 12, 1934, shipbuilding was temporarily stopped and, on the basis of the report of the investigation committee, new stability calculations were made. They proved that within the tonnage restrictions, no aircraft carrier with a fighting power worth mentioning could be built.[7] The Naval General Staff had to accept that excessive requirements had disastrous effects on shipbuilding technique if the naval architects complied with them. A new design had to be made. In this situation it was decided to abandon the "type-adverse" mounting of low-angle guns and to build the later-to-be-built *Sōryū* as a pure aircraft carrier. For this design the following parameters were required:

Standard displacement	10,050 tons	
Aircraft	18 + (6) fighters, 33 + (11) dive bombers, 51 + (17) in total	
Main engine	152,000 shp (same type as the heavy cruiser *Kumano*)	
Speed	35 knots	
Range	18 knots/7,800 miles	
Armament	12 12.7 cm high-angle guns in six twin mounts	
Protection	a) Magazine	Against 20 cm projectiles fired at ranges 12,000–20,000 m*
	b) Machinery spaces and gasoline tanks	Against destroyer armament (12.7 cm)

Note:

* Shorter range for vertical protection, longer range for horizontal protection because of the steeper angle of fall.

The drawings of basic design G 9 were completed at the end of October 1934. Comparison with the original design G 8 shows considerable changes that indicate the principal defects of the design made during that very progressive period of Japanese shipbuilding technology: a progress made without sufficient basic research and investigations about effects, and also not adequately resisting the pressure from the Naval General Staff.

A look at the next table reveals that length was reduced, draft was increased, the island bridge scaled down, the lateral plane reduced, the CG was lowered, stability range was increased, armament was modified, and curved funnels to starboard adopted.

Comparison of Designs G 6, G 8 and G 9			
Item / Design	Flying-deck cruiser G 6	Carrier-cruiser G 8	Aircraft carrier G 9
Standard displacement (tons)	approx. 12,000	10,050	15,900
Trial displacement (tonnes)	17,500	18,000	18,800
Length between perpendiculars (m)	?	223.02	206.52
Length at waterline (m)	240	240	222.0
Beam (m)	21.7	23.4	21.3
Draught (m)	6.3	6.265	7.62
Machinery, boilers	Kampon *Ro Gō* WTB oil burner × 8	Kampon *Ro Gō* WTB oil burner × 8	Kampon *Ro Gō* WTB oil burner × 8
Machinery, main engines	Kampon all-geared turbines × 4	Kampon all-geared turbines × 4	Kampon all-geared turbines × 4
Propeller shafts	4	4	4
Performance (shp)	150,000	150,000	152,000
Speed (knots)	36	35.5	34.5
Range (knots/miles)	18/10,000	18/10,000	18/7,680
Fuel, heavy oil (tons)	3,760	4,000	3,400
Complement	?	1,800	1,100
Armament	6 50 cal Type 3 20 cm guns in three twin turrets; 12 40 cal Type 89 12.7 cm HAGs in six twin mounts	5 60 cal Type 3 15.5 cm guns (1 III, 1 II turret); 12 40 cal Type 89 12.7 cm HAGs in six twin mounts; 28 Type 96 25 mm MGs in 14 twin mounts	12 40 cal Type 89 12.7 cm HAGs in six twin mounts; 28 Type 96 25 mm MGs in 14 twin mounts
Aircraft	70 (fighters and torpedo bombers, normal and reserve included)	72, among them 24 Type 90 fighters, 48 Type 89 torpedo bombers	57 + (16), among them 12 + (4) Type 96 fighters, 9 + (3) Type 97 torpedo bombers, 27 + (9) Type 96 dive bombers, 9 + (0) Type 97 reconnaissance planes
Protection	Side: 100–140 mm Deck: 35–40 mm	?	Side: 35–140 mm Deck: 40 mm
Flight deck length × beam (m)	194.22 × 29.0	233 × 40.3	216.9 × 26.0
Hangars	2 (upper and lower)	2 (upper and lower)	2 (upper and lower)
Aircraft elevators	2	3	3

Notes:
WTB = Water-tube boiler; HAG = High-angle gun; MG = Machine gun.
Source:
Fukui Shizuo: *Japanese Naval Vessels Illustrated, 1869–1945, vol. 3, Aircraft Carriers, Seaplane Tenders & Torpedo Boat & Submarine Tenders,* pp. 69, 97, 331, 333.

Kure Navy Yard officially began construction on November 20, 1934. When the later vice admiral (naval architect) Niwata Shōzō was transferred to Kure as shipbuilding inspector in July of that year, the dock had just been prepared for *Sōryū*'s construction. Because there were no structural changes, most of the already prepared parts could be used. On December 23, 1935, the aircraft carrier, whose construction was treated as a military secret, was launched, and it was completed on December 29, 1937; it was one year later than planned.[8]

After the failure of the conversion of *Akagi* and *Kaga* into carriers and the overloaded construction of *Ryūjō*, the Japanese carrier-building technology came to its temporary zenith with the fifth ship—*Sōryū*. However, this result was attained only on the basis of the experiences from *Hōshō* to *Ryūjō* and after passing a process—hard to understand from a technical point of view.[9] In its final version, *Sōryū* showed typical features of later designs, so it can be considered the first modern "light fleet"-type carrier of the IJN. However, as a medium-sized type, some drawbacks existed, and they were clearly recognized: (1) insufficient protection, (2) comparatively small number of aircraft, and (3) short range. All these drawbacks were common to all medium-sized carriers that followed. Of course, no other result could be expected because the basic design was basically unchanged. In addition, one must not forget that this result was obtained by exceeding the stated standard displacement by almost 60 percent.

That these "defects" were clearly recognized can be proven by the change to the Shōkaku class after the termination of the arms limitation treaties, and still later with the *Taihō*.

The former two periods provide answers to some of the questions in the "Introduction" and indicate that the IJN recognized this type as "ideal" only in the sense that a medium-sized type inevitably had to have defects, and that these had to be taken into the bargain unless a remarkable increase in the displacement was permitted. On the other hand, the change to a more powerful and better-protected aircraft carrier indicates that the principle of individual superiority again became predominant, and that parity with the United States was to be attained with the conversion of other warship types and large passenger ships.

Ship	Building Yard	Laid Down	Launched	Completed
Sōryō	Kure	11/20/1934	12/23/1935	12/29/1937
Hiryū	Yokosuka	7/8/1936	11/16/1937	7/5/1939

Proposals for the Improvement of Basic Design G 9: The Second Ship Is Not Built as a Sister Ship to *Sōryū*

The provisional no. 2 aircraft carrier in the Circle 2 Program (*Maru Ni Keikaku*) of 1934 was built according to the design of *Sōryū* (G 9) about one year after the type ship. As stated above, *Sōryū* had emerged as an aircraft carrier after passing two intermediate stages as a hybrid. However, the Naval General Staff required a revision of the design with regard to the total conversion of *Kaga* and the far-reaching modifications of *Sōryū*, which had to be carried out after the *Tomozuru* and 4th Fleet Incidents. Also, one has to remember that certain type-character "defects" had been detected; foremost among these was the lack of protection, which became a "deadly weak point" of the medium-type aircraft carrier, but it had been accepted with the premise that *Soryū*'s displacement should not be increased.

As a consequence, the later *Hiryū* was designed according to basic design number G 10 as a carrier that, in some respects, actually differed significantly from *Sōryū*. The modifications can be divided roughly into two groups: improved ship qualities, and improved aircraft facilities.

To the first group belonged

1. improvement of seaworthiness by heightening the freeboard at the bow and stern
2. improvement of maneuverability, particularly turning, by changing the type of rudder (*Sōryū* had two parallel arranged spade rudders angled outward)
3. reinforcement of the structural strength (rigidity) of the hull by using traditional riveting instead of electric welding in case of the longitudinal strength members, and some other important connections
4. increase of plate thicknesses of the shell plating and strength deck
5. application of three different frame spaces depending on the distribution of the stress curve
6. reinforcement of magazine protection
7. increase of range (actually not achieved)

The second group consisted primarily of

1. increase of the beam of the flight deck by 1 m (27 m instead of 26 m as in *Sōryū*)[10]
2. change of the position of the island bridge (to port and at about half the length instead of to starboard and at about the end of the forward one-third of the length as in *Sōryū*)[11]

To summarize: *Hiryū*, which is always referred to as the second modern aircraft carrier of the IJN, was newly designed on the basis of *Sōryū*, and only her machinery part was identical. Of course, the general arrangement differed only in the extent required by the modifications listed above, but by the change of principal dimensions, the lines of the hull had to be revised so that *Sōryū* and *Hiryū* were actually two different ships, and sisters only because of their common original design and (official) regulations. Irrespective of the increase of the standard displacement by 1,400 tons compared with *Sōryū*, it had the same weaknesses as pointed out earlier. However, they were later considered to be of secondary importance since they were suitable for rapid building. In the emergency situation shortly before the beginning of the Pacific War, and still more after half a year of fighting, rapid building attained predominance for aircraft carriers. In that situation and in view of the generally satisfactory results it had achieved, *Hiryū* was chosen as the prototype for the Unryū class, of which many ships should speedily be built in order to turn the tide.

However, before turning to the Unryū class, it may be convenient with regard to the questions in the "Introduction" to first refer to the aircraft carrier–building policy.

The Aircraft Carrier Shipbuilding Policy after the Termination of the Arms Limitation Treaties

After building the two medium-sized aircraft carriers *Sōryū* and *Hiryū*, the IJN changed its building policy to larger types, carrying more aircraft and being better protected, as stated above. These types were part of the Third and Fourth Naval Armament Replenishment Programs of 1937 and 1939, respectively. This tendency was continued in the Fifth Naval Armament Replenishment Program, which was to be started on April 1, 1942. The Naval General Staff wanted to have three aircraft carriers of the modified *Taihō* type, but the navy minister changed one to a modified *Hiryū* type. The next table shows the budget (in ¥) prepared for this program on July 19, 1941.

Item / Type	Mod. *Taihō* type (30,100 tons)	Mod. *Hiryū* type (17,100 tons)
Expenses for hull	49,500,000	36,000,000
Expenses for machinery	17,426,000	14,557,000
Total shipbuilding expenses (A)	66,926,000	50,557,000
Expenses for military equipment (B)	62,264,000	57,186,000
Total (A) + (B)	129,190,000	107,743,000
Administrative expenses	2,436,000	2,073,000
Total expenses/expenses per ton	131,626,000/4,373	109,816,000/6,421

Note:
Pay attention to the comparatively small difference of the total expenses and the big difference in costs per ton.

However, as will be explained later, the beginning of this program had to be postponed and totally revised after the defeat at the Battle of Midway. Therefore, it simply became a "paper program," just like the Sixth Naval Armament Replenishment Program, for which neither an exact calculated budget nor a building plan was executed.

According to vol. 31 of the official Japanese War History (*Kaigun Gunsenbi*, vol. 1), p. 607, the Sixth Naval Armament Replenishment Program "disappeared before the beginning of the investigation," but in some other sources it is said that three aircraft carriers of a still-larger type than *Taihō* (50,000 tons) were planned to be built. Even though in view of the then-existing tendency there are indications of high probability, it is only a supposition.

These few data make it obvious that the IJN did not consider the medium-sized carrier as the ideal type, but after the termination of the arms limitation treaty system it changed its building policy in the regular fleet replenishment programs to the larger type, representing an increase of offensive and defensive properties. While striving for individual superiority with these types, the primary goal, parity with the USN, was not given up but should be attained with "auxiliary" types.

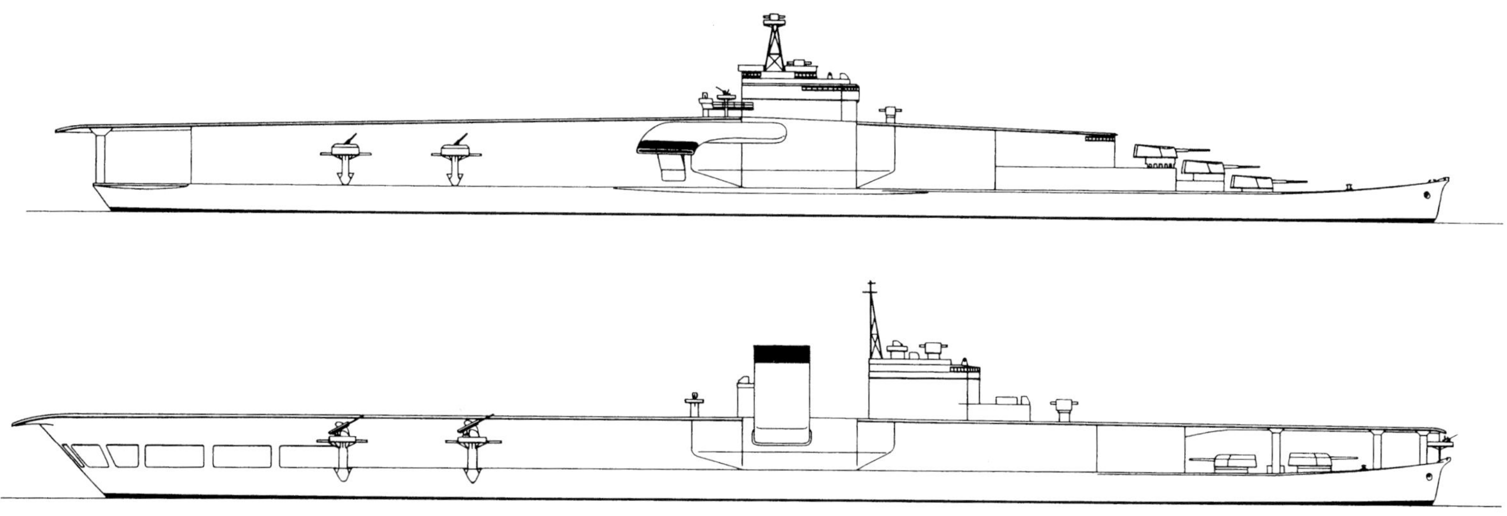

Designs G 6 (*top*) and G 8 (*bottom*). *Peter Mickel*

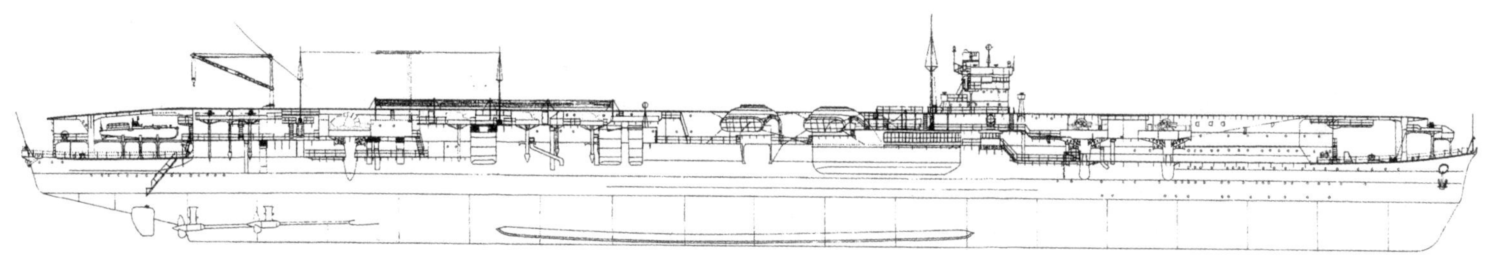

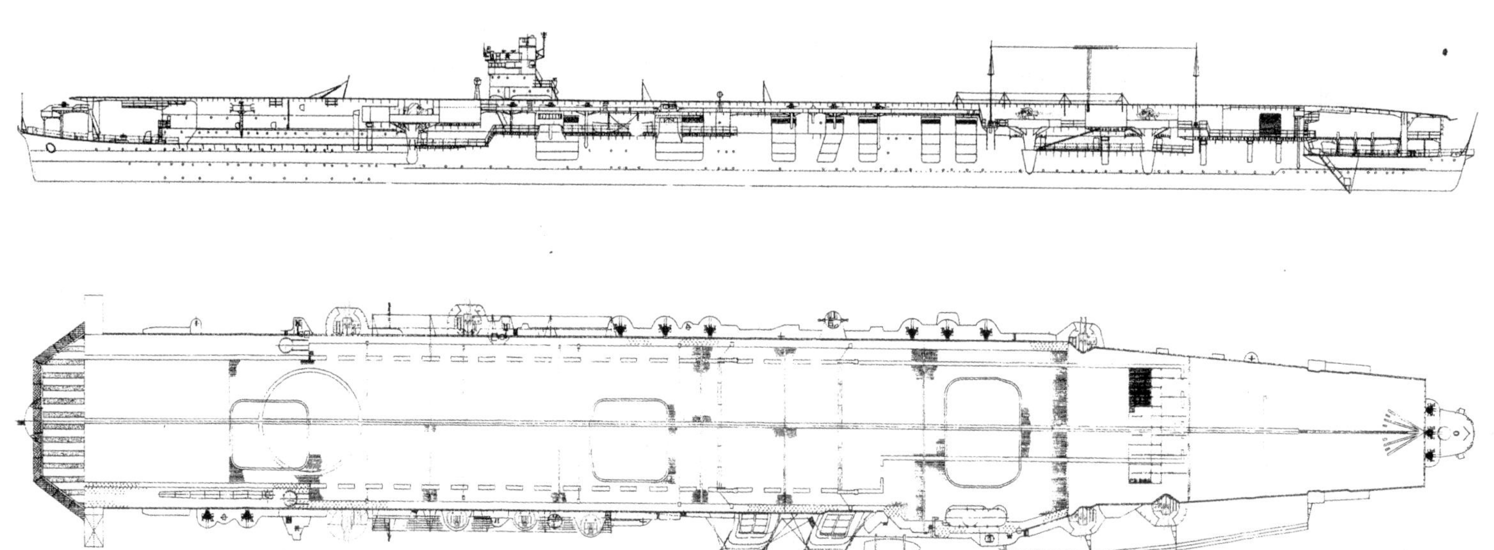

Sōryū. Jürg Tischhauser

Sōryū on December 23, 1935, at Kure Navy Yard dock no. 4. Note the elaborate decorations with a dragon on the bow. The large decorative ball (*kusudama*) has been broken. *Courtesy of Eugen Pinak*

Sōryū in Kure Navy Yard in the spring of 1937. Scantlings are erected, and the carrier is ready to be painted. Guns are not yet mounted.

Sōryū at Kure Navy Yard in the spring of 1937. The ship is being painted, and to the right is a 200-ton crane. Note her name in *hiragana.*

Sōryū immediately after delivery at Kure on December 29, 1937. She was incorporated into the 2nd *Kōkū Sentai* (Carrier Division), and although it is flying the flag of Rear Admiral Mitsunami Teizō, there are still unfinished parts.

Sōryū soon after delivery in late 1937 or early 1938, off Kure or Yokosuka. It is a slightly retouched photo, and it was the only photo of *Sōryū* released by the IJN.

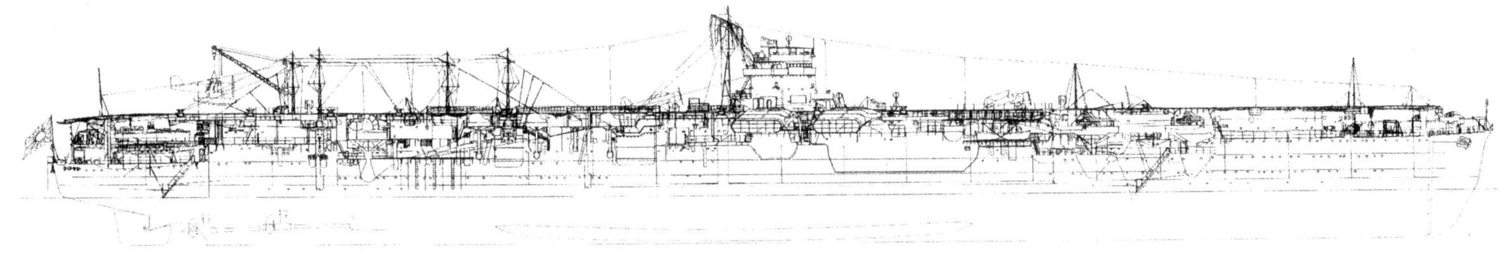

CV Hiryû

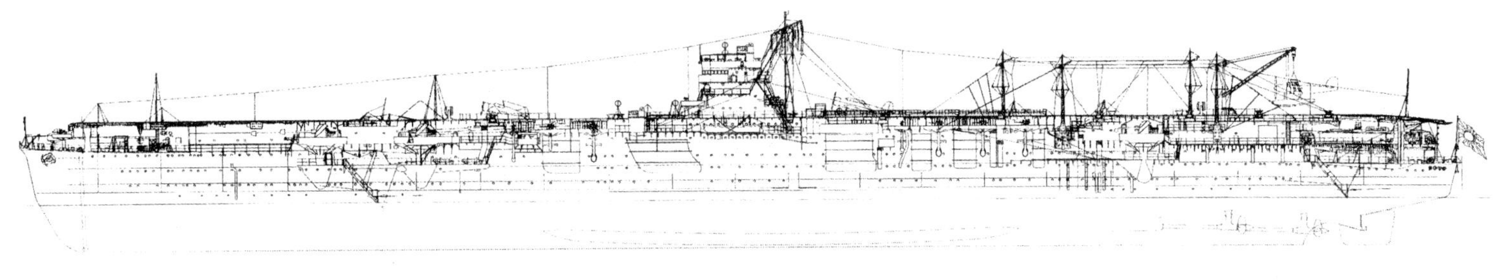

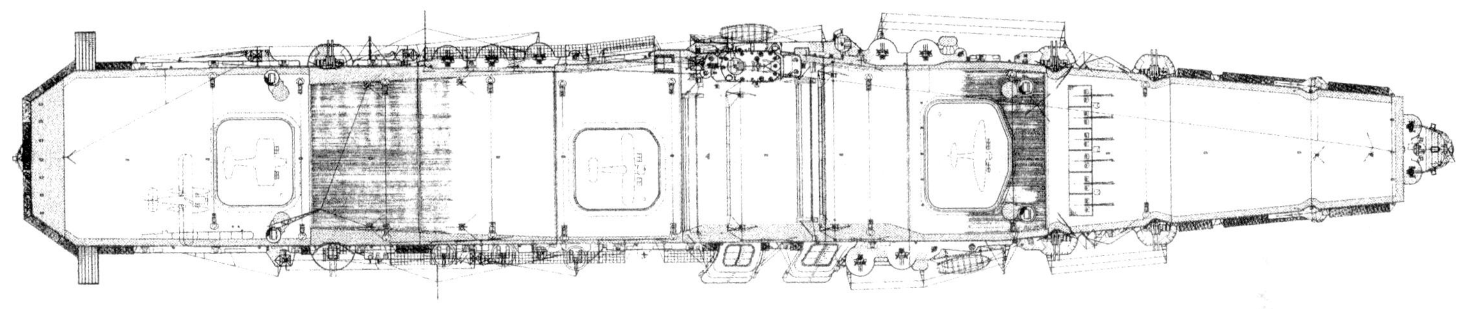

Hiryū. Jürg Tischhauser

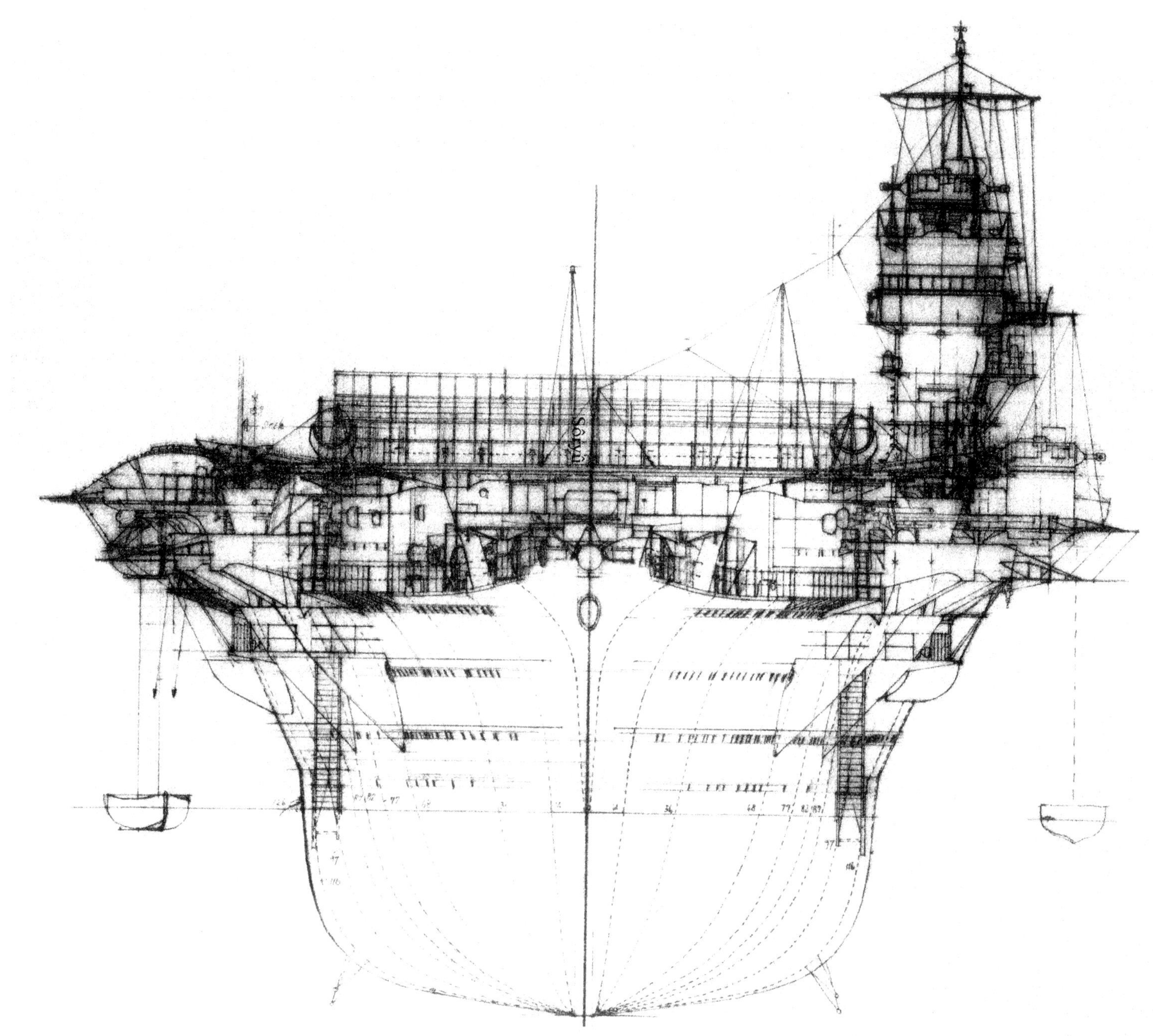

Bow view of *Hiryū. Pencil study by Jürg Tischhauser*

Stern view of *Hiryū. Pencil study by Jürg Tischhauser*

Launch of *Hiryū* at Yokosuka Navy Yard on November 16, 1937. The *kusudama* has been broken, and seven doves and confetti of five different colors are released. *Courtesy of Dan Kaplan*

Hiryū during her final outfitting on February 20, 1939, at Yokosuka Navy Yard's Koumi Basin. The aft elevator is being loaded with a 200-ton crane, and the funnel smoke tells us that the engines are working.

Hiryū running trials on the Iwafukuro–Ukishima mile off Tateyama on April 28, 1939. High-angle guns are mounted, but not machine guns and type 94 directors.

Another view of *Hiryū* off Tateyama on April 28, 1939. Note that her bridge structure is one deck higher than *Sōryū*'s.

Starboard view of *Hiryū* running trials off Tateyama on April 28, 1939. Trials began soon after construction, and the ship is rather dirty.

Hiryū under completion at Yokosuka Navy Yard on June 20, 1939. Ballast is being loaded, and the ship is being prepared for final trials.

CHAPTER 3

Concentration on the Medium-Sized Aircraft Carrier

The Wartime Warship Urgent Program: Aircraft Carrier *Unryū*[1]

In June 1940, the Third Vinson-Trammell Law (11 percent Fleet Expansion Bill) permitted the building of three aircraft carriers of the third generation: the Essex class (*Essex*, *Yorktown*, and *Intrepid*). In July of the same year, the United States suddenly announced the Stark Program (the Two-Ocean Fleet Program), which allowed the USN to build eight more Essex-class carriers, bringing the total to eighteen.

The IJN reacted with the previously stated Fifth and Sixth Naval Armament Replenishment Programs, began converting "concealed warships" into light aircraft carriers, and also put into effect the so-called Expeditionary Preparation Plan (*Shusshi Junbi Keikaku*), whose stage 1 (*dai ichi chaku*) came into force on November 15, 1940. The second stage was put into force on August 15, 1941, and this meant the building of warships according to the Wartime Program (*Senji Keikaku*) and the overall execution of the Expeditionary Preparation Plan. Under this plan the building of wartime warships was divided into three periods. In the first period, it was planned to reinforce the war preparations in all item shortages that had been recognized as compared with the USN, and to replenish those classes of warships whose attrition in wartime was forecasted.

The Wartime Warship Urgent Program (*Senji Kyūzō Kansen Kenzō Keikaku*), later called just the Urgent Program (*Maru Kyū Keikaku*), was included in the directions as a wartime program because it was to be carried out only when the decision for war had been made.[2] This program embraced 293 mostly small war vessels but also one aircraft carrier (the later *Unryū*), to improve rather quickly the ratio with regard to regular aircraft carriers. By planning only one aircraft carrier in this program, the IJN missed the chance to "quickly" build the medium-sized Unryū-class (basic design number G 16)—in "mass production."[3]

The Urgent Carrier Reinforcement Program: Planned Mass Production of Aircraft Carriers of the Modified *Unryū* Class

As a result of the Battle of Midway, an immediate and fundamental change of the shipbuilding policy became necessary. Four carriers, the main strength of the naval air force, were lost. Five of the ten carriers available at the beginning of the Pacific War were sunk in two sea battles in May and June 1942; the carrier strength was reduced to half after half a year of war. To cope with this situation, the Naval General Staff initiated a study to change the basic policy of armament and war production, having an increase of air strength and construction of aircraft carriers as its main objectives. On June 20–21, 1942, a conference on the improvement of the aircraft carrier, among other topics, took place aboard the flagship of the Combined Fleet, the battleship *Yamato*. On the basis of the results of this conference, the Navy Technical Department drafted a plan for the immediate construction of aircraft carriers and submitted it to the Bureau of Naval Affairs (Navy Ministry) and the Naval General Staff. This plan, which was known as Navy Secretariat Secret Document #8107, was approved by the navy minister on June 30, 1942, and, at the same time, its execution was directed.

The goal of the Urgent Aircraft Carrier Reinforcement Program,[4] as the proposal of the Navy Technical Department was called, was the building of twenty-nine aircraft carriers before the end of fiscal year 23 (March 31, 1949). Fourteen of these twenty-nine carriers were to belong to the medium-sized Unryū and modified Unryū classes,[5] so it is no exaggeration to state that main emphasis was laid upon this type.

The *Unryū* and Modified *Unryū* classes								
Building Yard	**Prov. Name**	**Name**	**Planned Beginning**	**Planned Completion**	**Actual Laying Down**	**Actual Launching**	**Actual Completion**	**Notes**
Yokosuka	#302	*Unryū*	7/1942	9/1944	8/1/1942	9/25/1943	8/6/1944	Taken over from *Maru Kyū Keikaku*
Nagasaki	#5001	*Amagi*	10/1942	12/1944	10/1/1942	10/15/1943	8/10/1944	
Yokosuka	#5002							Suspended owing to the conversion of *Shinano*. Not included in the official program
Kure	#5003	*Katsuragi*	2/1943	3/1945	12/8/1942	1/19/1944	10/15/1944	
Nagasaki	#5004	*Kasagi*	1/1943	6/1945	4/14/1943	10/19/1944	—	Fitted out in Sasebo Navy Yard; work suspended after laying down, official building stop 4/1/1945
Yokosuka	#5005							Vide #5002
Kure	#5006	*Aso*	3/1943	9/1945	6/8/1943	11/1/1944	—	Work suspended after laying down; official building stop 11/9/1944. Used for demolition tests
Kōbe	#5007	*Ikoma*	7/1943	10/1945	7/5/1943	11/17/1944	—	Official building stop 11/9/1944 Further use decided on 11/17/1944
Nagasaki	#5008	*Kurama*	11/1943	12/1945				Canceled
Yokosuka	#5009	—	7/1943	3/1946				Canceled
Nagasaki	#5010	—	4/1944	6/1946				Canceled
Yokosuka	#5011	—	6/1944	9/1946				Canceled
Kure	#5012	—	6/1944	9/1946				Canceled
Yokosuka	#5013	—	6/1944	3/1947				Canceled
Yokosuka	#5014	—	10/1944	9/1947				Canceled
Yokosuka	#5015	—	1/1956	3/1948				Canceled

This table shows that only three aircraft carriers were completed (*Unryū*, *Amagi*, and *Katsuragi*). The work on three more (*Kasagi*, *Aso*, and *Ikoma*) was stopped on the slipways, and the construction of the other eight was canceled. None of the completed ships carried the planned aircraft complement, and they took no part in any offensive operation.

As stated earlier, the *Hiryū* was taken as prototype (model), and the general directions given for the Unryū class consisted of the following:

1. simplification of the structure and equipment in order to reduce man-days and building period
2. modification of the aviation facilities for new types of aircraft
3. use of substitute materials

The following items were concrete requirements:

1. In contrast to *Hiryū*'s bridge, the position shall be to starboard at about the end of the forward one-third of the ship's length.
2. Instead of three elevators, only two shall be fitted and they shall be modified for new types of aircraft.
3. The rudder shall be changed from the semibalanced type of *Hiryū* to spade rudders arranged as in *Sōryū*.
4. The antiaircraft armament shall be increased.

Apart from modifications in other sectors, the Unryū class was built as the *Hiryū*, which, in turn, was a modified *Sōryū*, and this allows a common technical outline of the IJN's medium-sized aircraft carriers to be provided.

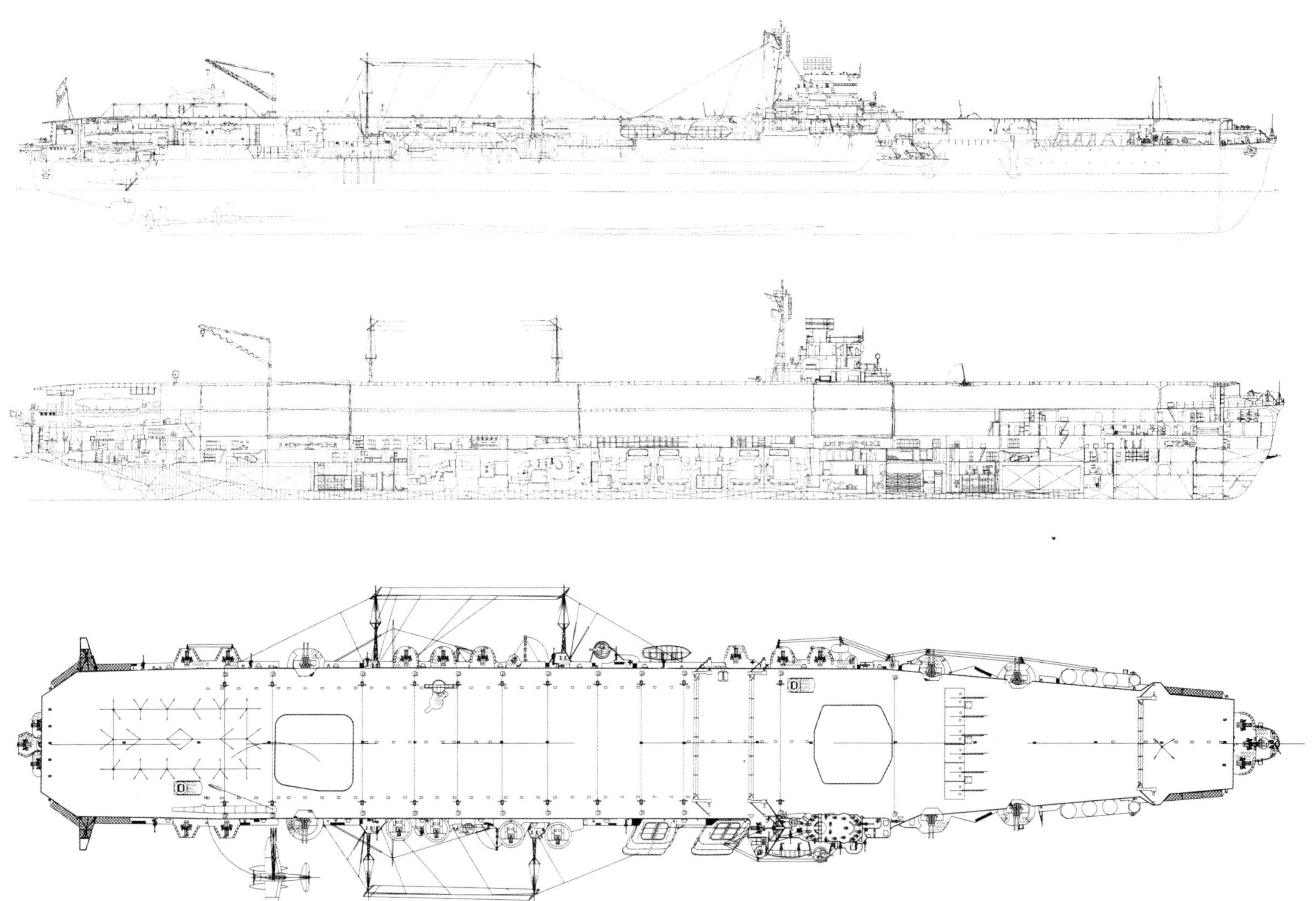

Unryū. Manfred Pasch

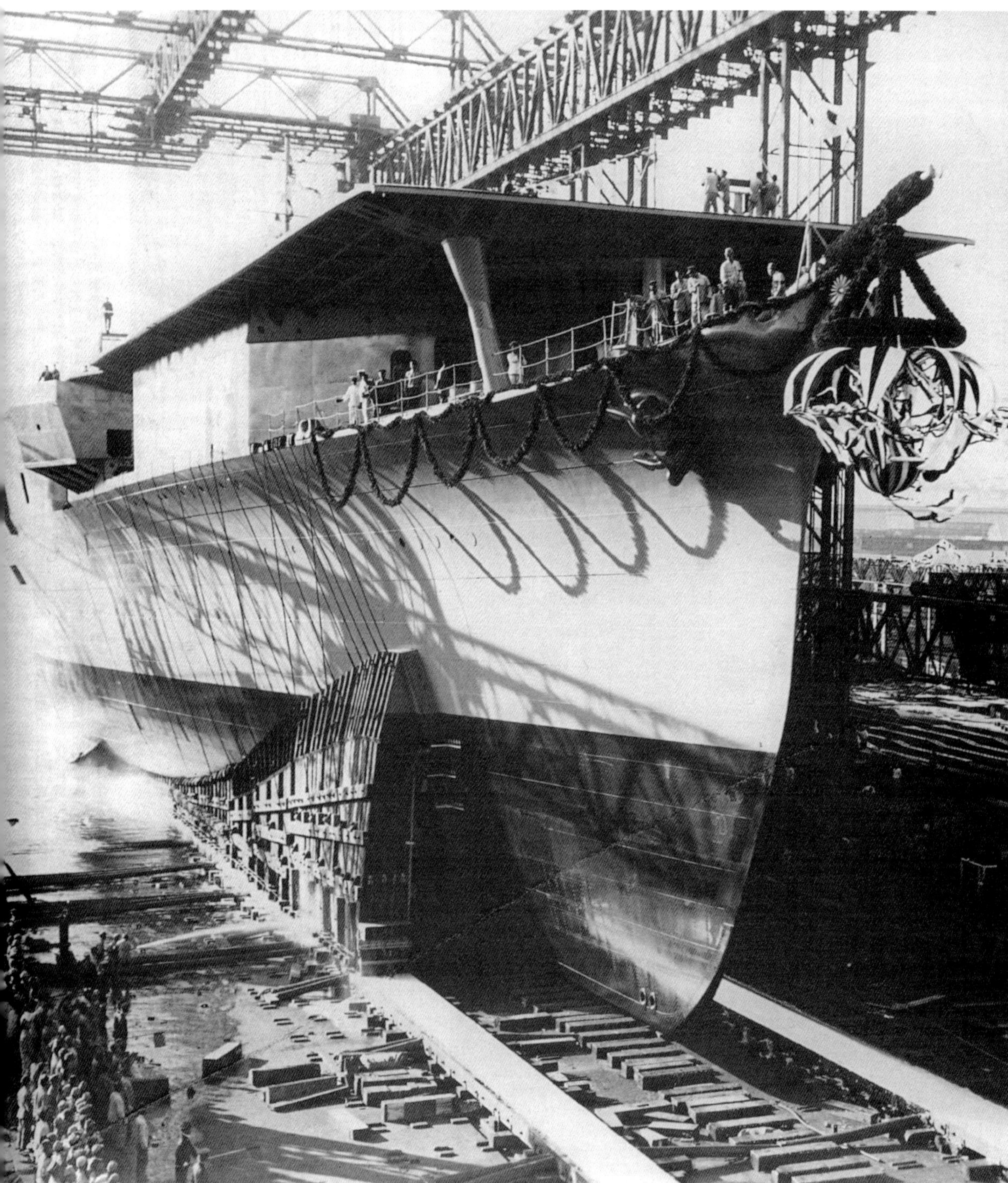

Unryū is launched at Yokosuka Navy Yard on September 25, 1943. For the first time, a Japanese carrier was launched with flight deck and hangars. *Sekai no Kansen*

Amagi at Kure in August 1944, just before completion. The island is different from *Unryū*, and two type 21 radars and one type 13 radar (signal mast) can be seen. One 110 cm searchlight is in a raised position aft. Moveable single 25 mm machine guns are forward of the island. The carrier also had six 12 cm rocket launchers. *Sekai no Kansen*

Katsuragi running the official mile between Sada-misaki and Kure in early October 1944. A type 21 radar is on the island, with shortened signal mast and camouflage painting.

The incomplete *Kasagi* in Ebisu Bay, Sasebo, on September 25, 1945. The submarine *Ha 217* is alongside, and to the right is the light carrier *Ibuki*.

CHAPTER 4

Outline Description

General Arrangement

A carrier can be characterized as a ship built around its aircraft complement, which enables the ship to exercise control over the sea and air space around the ship at the same time. The carrier as a ship and its main weapon, the aircraft, developed into a homogenous unit with unparalleled striking power, but also with a vulnerability to enemy weapons. The reason for this dichotomy was the air group itself, which dictated the general layout of the ship. With the building of the first medium-sized aircraft carriers, the IJN adopted a standard general arrangement that was set forth in all later types.

The largest spaces relating to area and volume were occupied above the waterline by two hangars arranged one above the other, and below the waterline by the machinery spaces, consisting mainly of the boiler rooms, the engine rooms, and the fore and aft generator rooms.

The hangars were divided into three sections (arranged as nos. 1–3), separated by the forward and middle aircraft elevator, while the aft elevator formed the after end of the no. 3 section. The Unryū*s* had only two elevators, and the aft one was not located as far aft as in *Sōryū* and *Hiryū*. Their hangars were divided into four sections (arranged as nos. 1–4), and nos. 2 and 3 were separated from the others by fire curtains instead of the middle elevator as in *Sōryū* and *Hiryū*.

The boiler rooms (BRs) and engine rooms (ERs) were separated by transverse bulkheads and a longitudinal bulkhead at the centerline in order to obtain eight rooms for eight boilers and four rooms for four all-geared turbine sets. This arrangement was regarded as being "ideal." The supply of steam of two boilers to one turbine set in normal operation, as well as a clever steam pipe arrangement permitting a quick shift to operating boilers and disconnecting of damaged ones, was thought to prevent immobilization. However, war lessons proved the danger of the longitudinal bulkhead and the traditional BR-BR-BR-BR-ER-ER arrangement was disadvantageous compared with the modern and flexible shift (BR-ER-BR-ER) system.

Below the flight deck and partly covered by it was the anchor deck, extending from the front of the upper hangar to the bows as a continuation of the upper hangar deck. The flight deck itself was the roof of the upper hangar.

At the aft end of the ship and likewise arranged as described above, but one deck height below (upper deck height), was the boat deck with the ship's boats, handled by overhead cranes (traveling on I beams fixed to the flight deck), stern anchor and mooring equipment, aircraft engine examination station, 12.7 cm loading-practice gun, 25 mm triple machine guns, and some minor equipment. Below, the upper deck was continued to the stern. Here, all equipment for anchoring (capstan and cable holders for stern anchor) and mooring was concentrated, and it was also the lower ship boat stowage.

The lower hangar was considerably shorter than the upper one because between the upper and lower hangar deck, the upper deck was fitted in front of no. 1 hangar section, and this space was used on both decks as living compartments for officers, crew's spaces, passageways, etc.

In the fantail the arrangement was similar but without reducing the length of no. 3 lower-hangar section, because in *Sōryū* and *Hiryū* the between deck (middle deck) began at the aft end of the after aircraft elevator. In the Unryūs, with the aft elevator located more forward, the upper- and lower-hangar aft sections were aft of the elevator, with that in the lower hangar shorter because one part was used for compartments. In this area there were living quarters for special-duty officers, crew's spaces, washrooms, toilets, and other living accommodations.

Between the outer hull plating and the side walls of the hangars, there were messes, standby rooms, and sleeping accommodations for the aviation personnel, and also standby rooms for the high-angle and machine gun personnel. Ventilation trunks, boiler uptakes, and ammunitions hoists were situated mainly outside the hangar walls, but they also "penetrated" to the inside in some cases.

The spaces at both sides of the aircraft elevators were used mainly for spare parts of aircraft, storerooms, maintenance of aircraft weapons, and motor rooms for the collapsible radio antennae masts, of which two were located on sponsons on each side.

Due to the aforementioned arrangement, the sides of the hangars were considerably irregular, with many protuberances, and the handling of aircraft was difficult work.

On the lower deck were living compartments for special-duty officers, crew's spaces, passageways, arrester gear engine rooms, crash barrier engine rooms, aircraft elevator pits with the elevator machinery, storerooms, shops, etc.

Below the lower deck the machinery spaces dominated, not only because of their volume but also because of their position in the central part of the ship. The forward and aft one-thirds of the length were divided into three and two floors, respectively, between the lower deck and the double bottom by the lowermost deck and hold at the fore, while in the aft one-third, only the lowermost deck was continued almost to the stern.

Forward of the boiler rooms were the forward generator and transformer room, the forward bomb magazine, the forward high-angle-guns ammunition magazine, and the 25 mm projectile magazine. Forward of the magazines were the structurally separated forward gasoline tank group and the forward trimming and heavy-oil tanks. Upon it there were crew's spaces, the anchor chain room, the capstan engine room, etc.

Aft of the boiler and engine rooms, the hull was divided likewise: the aft bomb magazine, the torpedo magazine, the high-angle guns and antiaircraft machine-gun ammunition magazines, the aft gasoline tank group, the aft trimming tank, the tiller room, watertight compartments, etc. In the Unryūs, the torpedo magazine was located forward of the machinery spaces, and here the combined bomb and torpedo hoist was also situated. This was contrary to the usual practice, but the authors have not yet found an explanation for this reversion.

Above the magazines and gasoline tank groups, there were living compartments and various other rooms necessary for operating the ship and its equipment.

This very rough description gives the impression that the general arrangement of Japanese and British aircraft carriers was rather similar, except for hangars, magazines, and gasoline tank groups. While the USN carriers usually had only one hangar, the IJN principally and also the RN often arranged an upper and lower hangar. They were of enclosed type in the IJN and RN, while the USN favored the open type. The standard arrangement below the lower deck was in Japanese carriers always in the following order: forward gasoline tank groups, forward ammunition magazines, forward bomb (and torpedo) magazines, forward generator and transformer room with pyrotechnic room above it, boiler rooms, engine rooms, aft bomb (and torpedo) magazines, aft ammunition magazines, and aft gasoline tank group. In contrast, the RN chose the following order: forward ammunition magazines, forward gasoline tank group, boiler rooms and engine rooms, aft gasoline tank group, and aft ammunition magazines. In this arrangement the gasoline tanks were located within the main protective area (as in the aircraft carriers of the USN) in order to have maximum protection. The IJN was guided by the idea to place this most dangerous substance for the ship outside the protected vital area—as much as possible toward the stem and stern. War lessons proved that this location was very dangerous (one should not forget that the beam of the hull was reduced at those locations) and much inferior to the arrangement preferred by the RN and the USN.

Stern view of *Sōryū* in November 1937. Waves are high and the roar of the sea must be deafening. The starboard helm signal (green ball) shows that the ship is not turning.

Hiryū during final stages of completion at Koumi Basin Yokosuka Navy Yard on May 20, 1939. She is being painted and prepared for delivery. Battleship *Mutsu* is behind.

Katsuragi likely leaving Mitsugojima. *Sekai no Kansen*

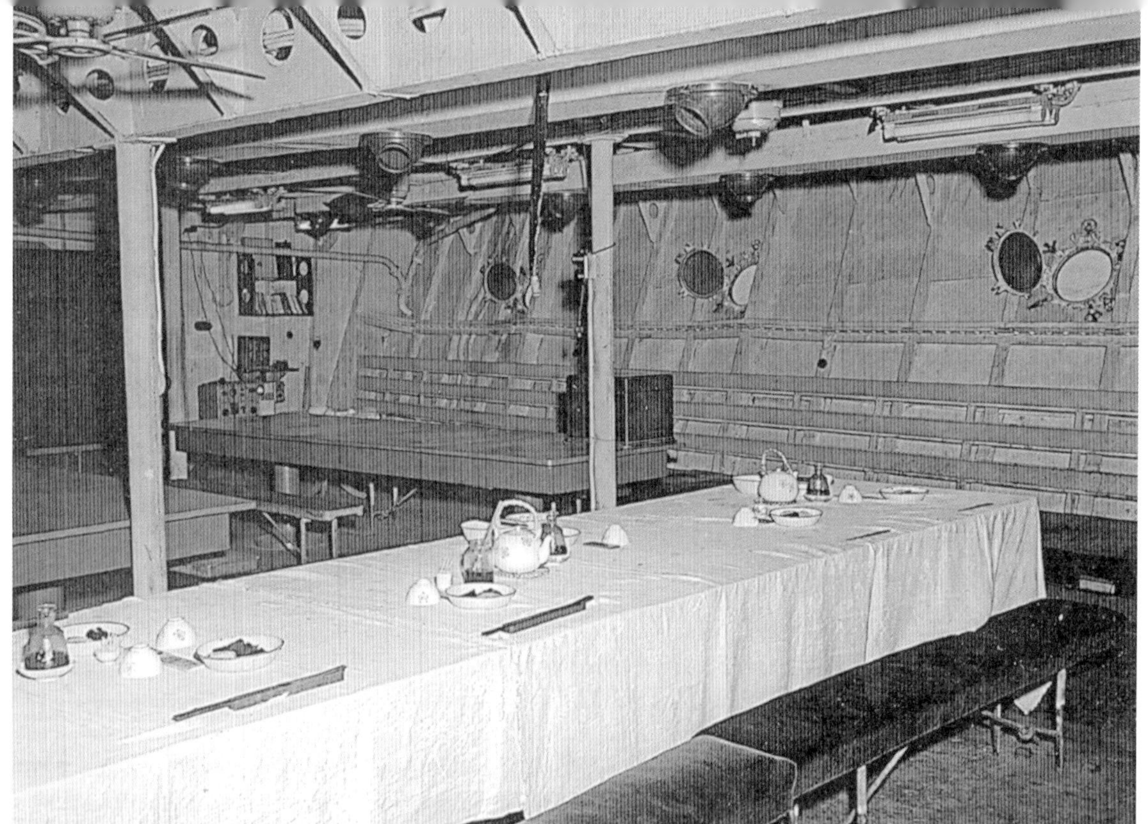

Probably the officer's mess on *Katsuragi*, but the table cloth is questionable. *US National Archives*

Looking aft into *Katsuragi's* hangars. *Courtesy of Dan Kaplan*

CHAPTER 5

Hull with Appendages

Principal Dimensions, Coefficients and Ratios, Form of Stem and Stern, Frames, Depth, Draft, and Freeboard

The principal dimensions and their influence are explained in the following pages.

Principal Dimensions				
Item/Ship	***Sōryū***	***Hiryū***	***Unryū* + #302 Class**	***Ikoma* (mod. #302 class)**
Length, overall (m)	227.00	227.00	227.35	227.35
Length, waterline (m)	222.00	222.93	223.00	223.00
Length, between perpendiculars (m)	206.52	206.52	206.52	206.52
Beam, waterline (m)	21.30	22.00	22.00	22.00
Depth, keel to flight deck (m)	20.50	20.50	20.50	20.50
Trial displacement (tons)	18,800	20,250	20,100	20,450
Draft, trial displacement, forward (m)			7.48	7.58
As above aft (m)			8.03	8.04
As above mean (m)	7.40	7.50	7.76	7.86
Full-load condition (tons)		21.887	21.779	22.005
Draft, full-load condition (m)		8.21	8.13	8.20
Standard displacement (tons)	15,900	17.300	17.150	17.500
Length of flight deck (m)	216.90	216.90	216.90	216.90
Width of flight deck, forward (m)	16.00	16.00	16.00	16.00
As above maximum (m)	26.00	27.00	27.00	27.00
As above aft (m)	17.00	17.00	17.00	17.00
Oil fuel capacity (full load) (tons)	3,400	3,750	3,750	3,750
Range (knots/miles)	18/7,800	18/7,670	18/8,000	18/7,800
Speed (knots)	35	34.3	34	34
Machinery output (shp)	152,000	153,000	152,000	152,000

Note:
According to Lt. Tōyama, Engineer Imai, and Assistant Engineers Takahashi & Ogino, "Weight of center of gravity data for miscellaneous warships by preliminary design group," second corrected and added edition, October 1941, p. 22, the displacements of *Sōryū* (*Hiryū*) were as follows: full load, 19,924.9 (21,751.7); trial, 18,447.7 (20,096.9); normal, 16,545.0 (17,980.7); light load, 14,632.3 (16,035.5).

Ratios and Coefficients					
Item/Ship	***Sōryū***	***Hiryū***	***Katsuragi***	**Average of CVs**	**CA *Tone***
RATIOS					
Lwl/Bwl (Length-to-beam ratio)	10.428	10.091	10.136	9.924	10.21
Bwl/d (Beam-to-draft ratio)	2.878	2.933	2.774	2.901	2.96
Lwl/D (Length-to-depth ratio)	11.82	10.878	10.878		18.165
D/d (Depth-to-draft ratio)	2.77	2.733	2.585		1.682
d/Lwl (Draft-to-length ratio)	0.0334	0.0338	0.0355	0.0349	0.0314
COEFFICIENTS					
Block coefficient (Cb)	0.502	0.5065	0.52	0.502	0.543
Prismatic coefficient (Cp)	0.590	0.592	0.60	0.579	0.6082
Amidships section coefficient (Cm)	0.851	0.856	0.86	0.867	0.8922
Waterline coefficient (Cw)	0.728	0.720	0.73	0.717	0.726

Notes:

1. The block coefficient is the ratio between the volume of displacement and that of a rectangular block whose edges are equal to the length, beam, and draft, respectively.
2. The prismatic coefficient is the ratio between the volume of displacement and that of a cylinder with the same length as the ship and a cross section equal to the area of the amidships section (f) below the designed waterline (A f).
3. The amidships section coefficient is the ratio between A f and a rectangle with sides equal to beam and depth.
4. The waterline coefficient is the ratio between the area of designed waterline and the circumscribing rectangle.
5. Data of heavy cruiser *Tone* stated for comparison

An outstanding characteristic is the large length-to-beam ratio. The principal reason was to attain speed and still maintain a reasonable machinery power, but in case of aircraft carriers, the length of the flight deck was also an important item. Generally speaking, a ship with a large L/B ratio is easy to keep on course, while transverse stability and maneuverability are influenced somewhat negatively.

A rather small beam-to-draft ratio is favorable for reducing hull resistance but generally exerts a negative influence on stability in stormy seas and high waves.

One more feature is the low amidships coefficient as a consequence of a rather large bilge radius in comparison with a large dead rise. In *Hiryū* it was 1.5 m (at Bwl/2 = 11.0 m). The slack amidships section was also the reason for the small beam-to-draft ratio.

The longitudinal coefficient was not large when compared with the speed–length ratio (√Lwl), which was 1.4 for *Katsuragi*. Both coefficients were the logical consequence of the large length-to-beam ratio because they also reduce hull resistance and support speed.

The IJN's designers preferred to locate the center of buoyancy in high-speed ships about 5 percent of the ship's length aft of amidships, although none but *Katsuragi* actually reached this value.

The coefficients and ratios of the heavy cruiser *Tone*, a ship designed at about the same time as *Hiryū*, are given for the sake of comparison. They are helpful to explain that the shape of the medium-sized aircraft carriers was that of high-speed ships. The adoption of the cruiser-type hull for aircraft carriers had begun with the *Hōshō* (5,500-ton-class light cruisers) and the *Ryūjō* (7,100-ton Aoba class) and was continued in these ships in enlarged form. On this hull, two hangars were built as the principal "superstructure."

Freeboard				
Item/Ship	***Ryūjō***	***Sōryū***	***Hiryū***	***Katsuragi***
Length, waterline (m)	175.386	222.00	222.93	223.00
Draft (m)	6.530	7.62	7.74	7.93
Displacement (tonnes)	12.574	18,000	19,860	18.444
Speed (knots)	30	34.5	34	32.7
Freeboard, forward (m)	6.970	7.780	8.740	
Freeboard, amidships (m)	3.970	8.080	7.960	
Freeboard, aft (m)	2.970	5.780	5.260	

Notes:

1. These values refer to the height of the upper deck above the trial waterline and not the flight deck.
2. Since it is an acknowledged fact that *Hiryū's* freeboard forward was 1 m higher, while aft the freeboard was higher by 0.4 m, Mr. Fukuda must have reversed the freeboard aft for *Sōryū* and *Hiryū*.

Source:

Fukuda Keiji, *Gunkan Kihon Keikaku Shiryō* (Tokyo: Konnichi no Waidasha, 1989), p. 33.

Another peculiarity of the hull form was the large cutting away of the fore foot, resulting in a bow shape tending toward the "Maier type."[1] This bow shape was typical of Japanese ships of that period and may also be described as curved into a gentle "S shape" with a considerable overhang at the stem. The reason for this shape was the use of the type 1 mine B (*Ichi Shiki Kirai Otsu*), developed shortly after the Russo-Japanese War, which was laid in the path of the US battle fleet immediately before the final phase of the decisive battle. The enemy was to be lured into a large field of connected mines, so it became necessary to give Japanese ships a bow shape, permitting them to run over the mines without actuating them. Even though the use was already considered impractical at that time, the shape of the bow was maintained.

The deadwood aft was cut away to obtain better propulsion and also to assist in turning, the latter generally somewhat unsatisfactorily. The length from the aft perpendicular to the aft keel knuckle was determined by docking and other practical factors.

The shape of the stern resembled the transom type. The stern contour plate had an "overhang," which was rounded in *Sōryū* and *Hiryū* but was sharply knuckled in the Unryūs. The distinct knuckle was an improvement.

The shape of the frames was characterized by the large dead-rise-and-bilge radius, as well as the large flare in the upper part, to provide sufficient beam for hangars and flight deck. Frame space varied in consideration of the stress. While *Sōryū* still had the traditional bipartite arrangement, three different spaces were, for the first time in an carrier, used in *Hiryū* and were maintained in the Unryūs: 600 mm at stem and stern, 900 mm next to them, and 1,120 mm (1,200 mm in *Sōryū*) amidships. The use of smaller frame spaces forward and aft became standard practice in Japanese warship design thereafter.

Depth from baseline to flight deck amidships was 20.50 m; from trial waterline to flight deck, 12.66 m (*Hiryū*) and 12.57 m (*Katsuragi*), respectively. This depth was sufficient to build two hangars one upon another, as stated earlier. It had been recognized that the higher the flight deck above the waterline, the better for flight operations. On the basis of experiences with *Ryūjō* and *Sōryū*, the height should be at least 12 m, and this goal was attained. On the other hand, the ratio of the lateral plane above and below waterline, which affects stability and was taken up as an important factor after the capsizing of the torpedo boat *Tomozuru*, is determined mainly by the draft and depth from the waterline to the flight deck. Also, the freeboard is the main value of the reserve buoyancy, which, in turn, is a decisive factor for the range of stability. Consequently, it was chosen as large as possible by considering every factor. As shown above, the depth-to-draft ratio (D/d) was 2.585, the ratio of the lateral plane above/below the waterline was 1.736 in *Katsuragi*.

The wetted surface is given by Fukuda as 5,106.39 m^2 and 5,241.118 m^2 for *Sōryū* and *Hiryū*, respectively.

Hull Weights of *Sōryū* and *Hiryū*				
Item/Ship	***Sōryū***		***Hiryū***	
Outer plating*	1,102.5/1,674.8	20.8	1,296/1,740.7	19.4
Frames*	250/304.5	3.8	355/432.9	4.8
Longitudinals*	436/695.2	7.4	590/842.0	9.4
Inner bottom plates*	351/352.0	4.4	385/370.4	4.1
Beams*	139/278.7	3.5	155/372.8	4.2
Pillar	11.7/11.3	0.1	12/24.9	0.3
Steel deck*	607/1,760.0	21.9	615/1,786.4	19.9
Bridge	18/17.9	0.2	40/23.4	0.3
Casing & smoke passage	160/179.9	2.2	197/214.9	2.4
Bulkheads*	570/823.5	10.3	600/1,018.3	11.3
Engine bed, boiler bed, etc.	216.6/270.6	3.4	225/332.2	3.7
Gun supports	67/89.6	1.1	100/140.8	1.6
Large forgings & castings	114.8/120.8	1.5	165/163.9	1.8
Wooden deck*	/2.3	—	30/—	—
Deck flooring*	27/22.4	0.3	110/22.2	0.2
Lining & partitions	95/97.4	1.2	/131.1	1.5
Heat insulation (e.g., magazines)	34.5/36.3	0.5	60/38.9	0.4
Angle bar used with protective members	59/61.5	0.8	80/79.2	0.9
Paint*	120/235.9	2.9	140/207.0	2.3
Superstructure above strength deck	/1,0981	13.7	/1,031.2	11.5
Ballast (?)	250/—	—	125/—	—
* Weight W 1	/6,049.3	75.3	/6.792.7	75.6
Weight W 2	/1,983.4	24.7	/2,180.5	24.4
Total	7,911.4/8,032.7	100	8,690/8.973.2	100

Source:
Fukuda, *Gunkan Kihon Keikaku Shiryō*. Behind "/," "Weight of center of gravity data for miscellaneous warships" by the Preliminary Design Group, Lt. Tōyama, Engineer Imai, and Assistant Engineers Takahashi & Ogino, second corrected and expanded edition, October 1941, p. 21. The latter data is probably correct.

Propellers, Rudders, Rudder Steering, and Bilge Keels

In *Sōryū* and the Unryūs, the four three-bladed propellers had a diameter of 3,900 mm (D).[2]

When *Hiryū* was designed, the type of rudder and its arrangement were changed. *Sōryū* had two balanced spade rudders, situated side by side and angled 18.5° outward. This type of rudder had been developed by the Naval Technical Research Institute (*Kaigun Gijutsu Kenkyūshō*) in order to reduce heeling due to the effect of the centrifugal force during turning. The results of *Sōryū* were good but were disappointing in the case of the destroyers *Ariake* and *Yūgure* (reducing the speed by 1.5 knots). When the destroyers were equipped with a semibalanced type (*han heikō shiki*), the results were good.[3] The Navy Technical Department believed that it was possible to improve the turning qualities by fitting one semibalanced rudder, rather than two spade rudders, and designed *Hiryū* with this type, also requiring, of course, a modification of the shape of the underwater body in that part. When the official trial took place, the result did not meet the expectations because advance and tactical diameters were too large at small rudder angles. Because *Hiryū*'s new attempt proved unsuccessful, *Sōryū*'s style was again adopted, and two spade rudders were installed in the Unryūs. The background to the change was not only improvement of turning qualities but also the belief that spade rudders were simpler to install than semibalanced ones.

The two-spade-rudder system functioned well in large warships but was a failure in destroyers. The single semibalanced rudder, established as a countermeasure, obtained good results in destroyers but failed in large warships. These contrary results explain the difficulties of scientific technology, but as a matter of fact, the relations were not investigated and studied sufficiently.

The rudder area of *Hiryū* was 30.51 m^2; for both rudders of the Unryūs, 26.8 m^2. The figure for the Unryūs was 1.64 % of the area.

All ships were equipped with electrohydraulic steering gears. There were two power plants for each steering unit. Besides the electrohydraulic steering gears, emergency control of the rudder(s) was furnished.

Large bilge keels were fitted to reduce the angle of heel and damp the period of roll. The bilge keels of *Hiryū* and the Unryūs had a length of 75.42 m, or 33.82% of the Lwl.[4] The width was 1.8 m. Bilge keels were not filled with filling material, but the interior was painted with a protective paint similar to bitumastic and was divided by bulkheads about 30 m apart.

Stability

Stability Values of *Sōryū* and *Hiryū*

Name	***Sōryū***				***Hiryū***			
Condition	Trial	Full load	Light load	Suppl. light load	Trial	Full load	Light load	Suppl. light load
Item								
Displacement	18,800	20,295	14,998.9	15,788.9	20,250	21,887	16,270	16,495
Draft (m)	7.62	8.03	6.52	6.75	7.84	8.28	6.70	6.76
KG (m)	8.35	8.16	9.41	9.01	8.27	8.08	9.25	9.17
GM (m)	1.63	1.78	0.69	1.05	1.81	2.01	0.96	1.05
OG (m)	0.73	0.13	2.89	2.26	0.43	- 0.21	2.65	2.47
Range (°)	100	110	91.5	98	109.6	110.7	96.3	97.8
GZ (m)	1.96	2.06	1.135	1.485	2.30	2.38	1.65	1.71
A/Aw	1.765	1.60	2.28	2.16	1.71	1.59	2.23	2.18
Ballast (tons)				WB 800				
Statical capsize angle (°)					52.5	51.6	53.6	53.6

Notes:
1. KG = height of center of gravity (G above keel [K])
2. GM = metacentric height; the vertical distance between the center of gravity (G) and the metacenter (M)
3. OG = height of center of gravity (G) above waterline (O)
4. Range = range of stability; range of inclination to either side of the equilibrium position through which the ship remains statically stable; beyond angle of maximum righting lever (GZ) ship in increasing danger of capsizing.
5. A/Aw = ratio of lateral plane above and below the waterline
6. WB = water ballast

Source:
Fukuda Keiji, *Gunkan Kihon Keikaku Shiryō*, p. 79, handwritten notes of Technical Vice Admiral Niwata Shōzō.

The stability lessons learned from the findings of the committee investigating the capsizing of the torpedo boat *Tomozuru*[5] were incorporated into the original design of *Hiryū*, while *Sōryū*'s design was revised.

Katsuragi had a period of roll of 14.8 seconds, same as *Hiryū*. This was 0.5 seconds below the mean value of the IJN's aircraft carriers. The designers accepted values between thirteen and fifteen seconds but for the most part obtained slightly more than fifteen seconds, as expressed by the sixteen seconds of *Sōryū* shown in the table.

Period of Roll

Name	Displacement	GM	Period of Roll	K	Beam, wl	K/Bwl
Sōryū	18,372	1.478	16	9.7	21.3	0.455
Hiryū	20,160	1.741	14.8	9.73	22.0	0.442

Source:
Fukuda Keiji, *Gunkan Kihon Keikaku Shiryō*, p. 84.
Note:
K = radius of gyration of the ship about a longitudinal axis through the center of gravity (G)

In high-speed ships, the use of full helm results in large angles of heel, which are disadvantageous not only with regard to stability but also for evasion of torpedoes and bombs and for fire control. Therefore, an additional consideration used in determining acceptable initial stability was the angle of heel during high-speed turns. The relationships among GM, KG, and the remaining elements, especially the turning circle, affecting the heel angle during a turn, had to be adjusted so that GM was able to limit the angle to 9°. As shown in the table, this value was exceeded in *Sōryū* but was attained in *Hiryū* and again was exceeded in *Katsuragi*.

Island Structure

Originally the small aircraft carrier *Hōshō* had an island bridge, but it was soon removed. With *Sōryū*, the IJN reintroduced it. It was located on a bulge of the flight deck to starboard and about 0.3 length from the bow. It was very small and contained only the most necessary compartments and equipment for navigation and control of flight operations.

Hiryū had her island bridge to port, something that it had in common with the rebuilt *Akagi*. After trials aboard, *Akagi* pilots objected to this position and preferred the starboard position. However, it was too late to change the position aboard *Hiryū*. Compared with *Sōryū*, the bridge was larger, and because of the position amidships, it was also one deck higher. Therefore the forward view was improved, as was also the all-around view.

The islands of the Unryūs had four decks, including the flight deck level. The reduction of one deck height compared with *Hiryū* was compensated for by the increased length of the island and by the increase in the number of sponsons to make room for the installation of newly developed equipment and weapons. The islands of the completed ships differed from each other in details.

When members of the Air Technical Intelligence Group inspected *Katsuragi* on October 26, 1945, they found that the island structure, though fairly crowded, was reasonably well laid out, and they noted in particular that there were no boiler uptakes in the island, that great attention was paid to visual lookouts, with many high-powered binoculars being provided, and that among the items of equipment in the navigating (compass) bridge was a small radar receiver with an "A" scope display (for the #21 radar fitted atop the bridge). One defect noted was that there was no control location where radar information was plotted, and that each operator telephoned his information to the bridge.

Heel Angles

Name/Item	Displacement	Speed	Ar	Am/Ar	DA/Lwl	DT/Lwl	Heel Angle
Sōryū	18,359	33		60.1		4.33	10.5
Hiryū	19,860	33.1		52.26		4.22	
Hiryū	20,163	33.2	30.56	52.2		5.18	9
Katsuragi	18,512	32		55.3	3.55	3.93	11

Note:
Ar = rudder area, Am = lateral middle line area, DA = advance, DT = transfer

Source:
Fukuda Keiji, *Gunkan Kihon Keikaku Shiryō*, p. 124, for *Katsuragi:* Official Ship Data Book.

Sōryū at Kure Navy Yard dock no. 3 in the autumn of 1937. Note the "Maier bow."

Stern view of *Sōryū* during trials in November 1937. Note the lifebuoy and the wake.

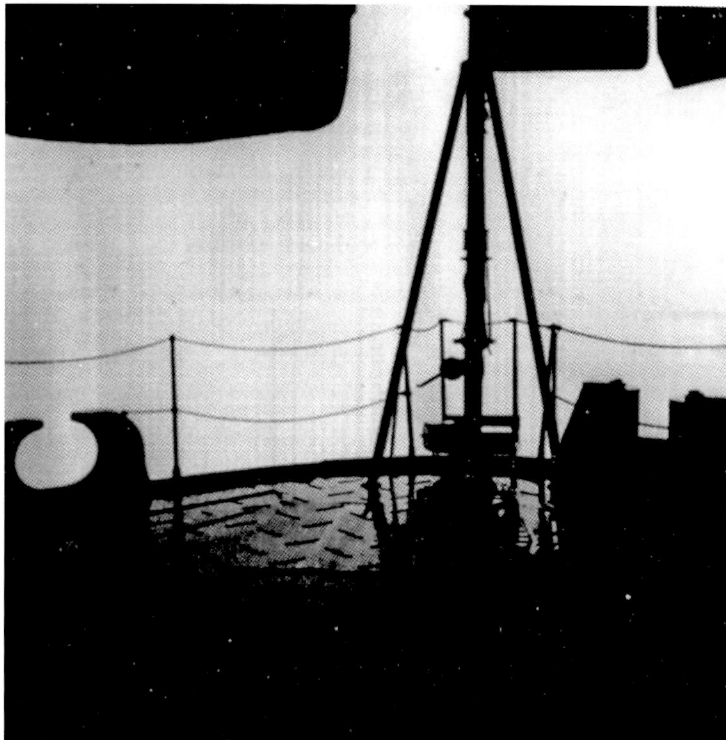

Hiryū's quarterdeck, showing the checker plate. *Courtesy of Nakagawa Tsutomu*

Sōryū during trials between Bungo Strait and Sukumo in November 1937. A view from above at the support of no. 3 (the second on the starboard side) high-angle gun.

View looking forward along *Katsuragi*'s port side. Note the simplified shape of the sponsons and the supporting struts. To the right is an emergency rudder. *US National Archives*

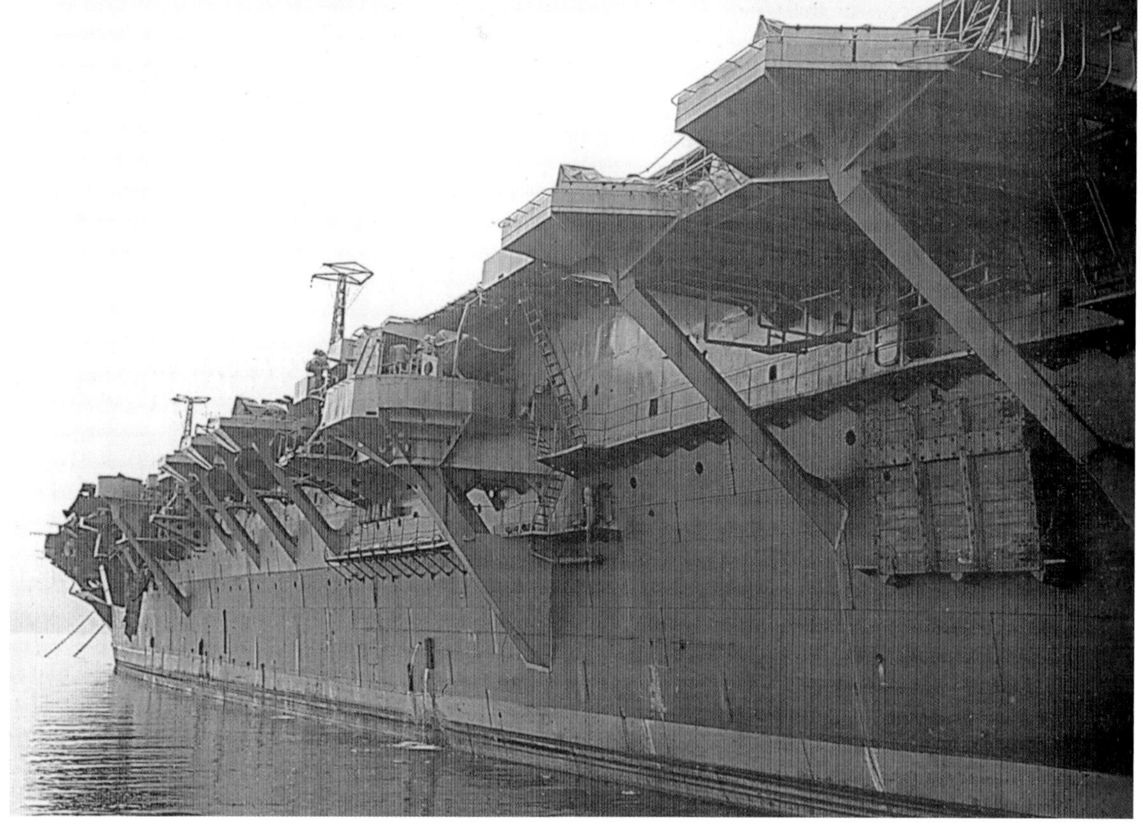

Kasagi on August 31, 1946. Note that she has a slight starboard list due to flooding. *Courtesy of Eugen Pinak*

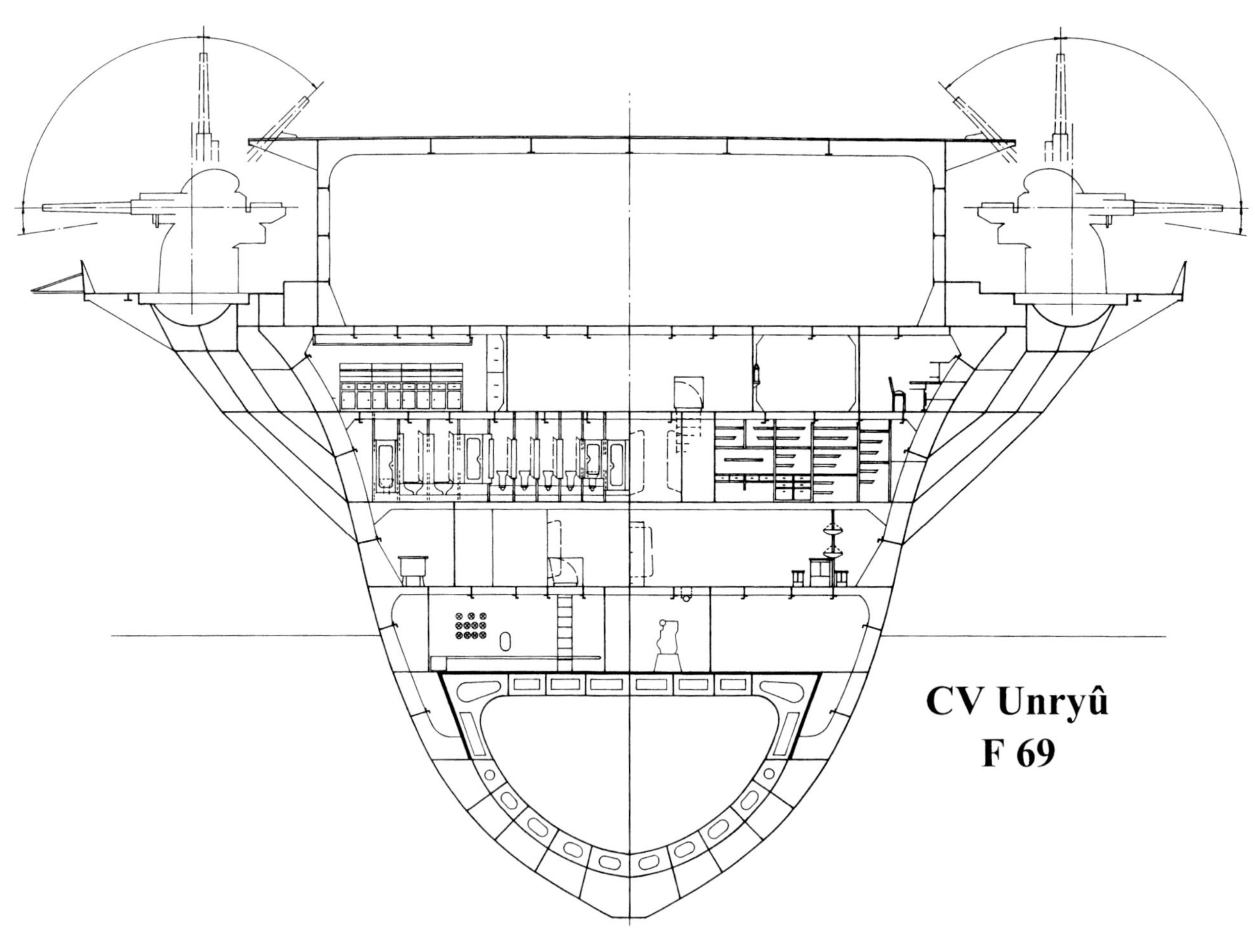

Sections of *Unryū*. *Jürg Tischhauser*

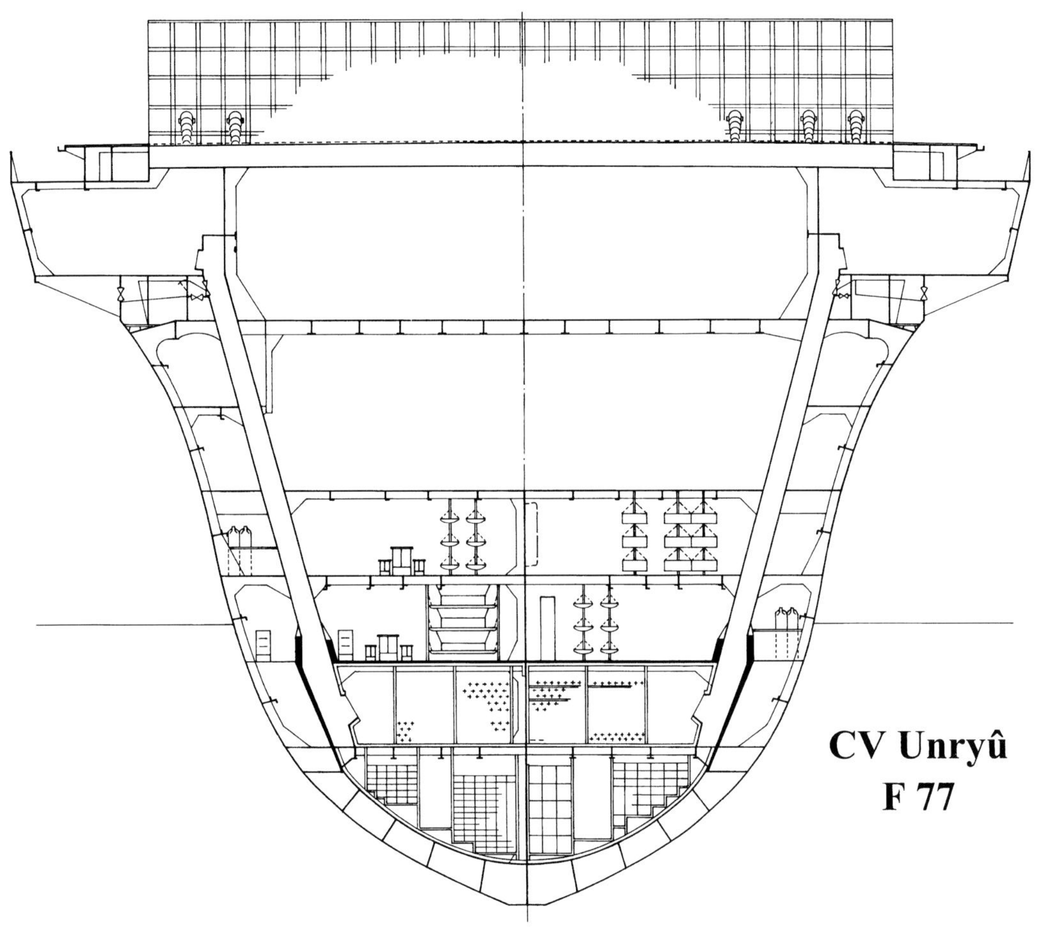

Sections of *Unryū*. *Jürg Tischhauser*

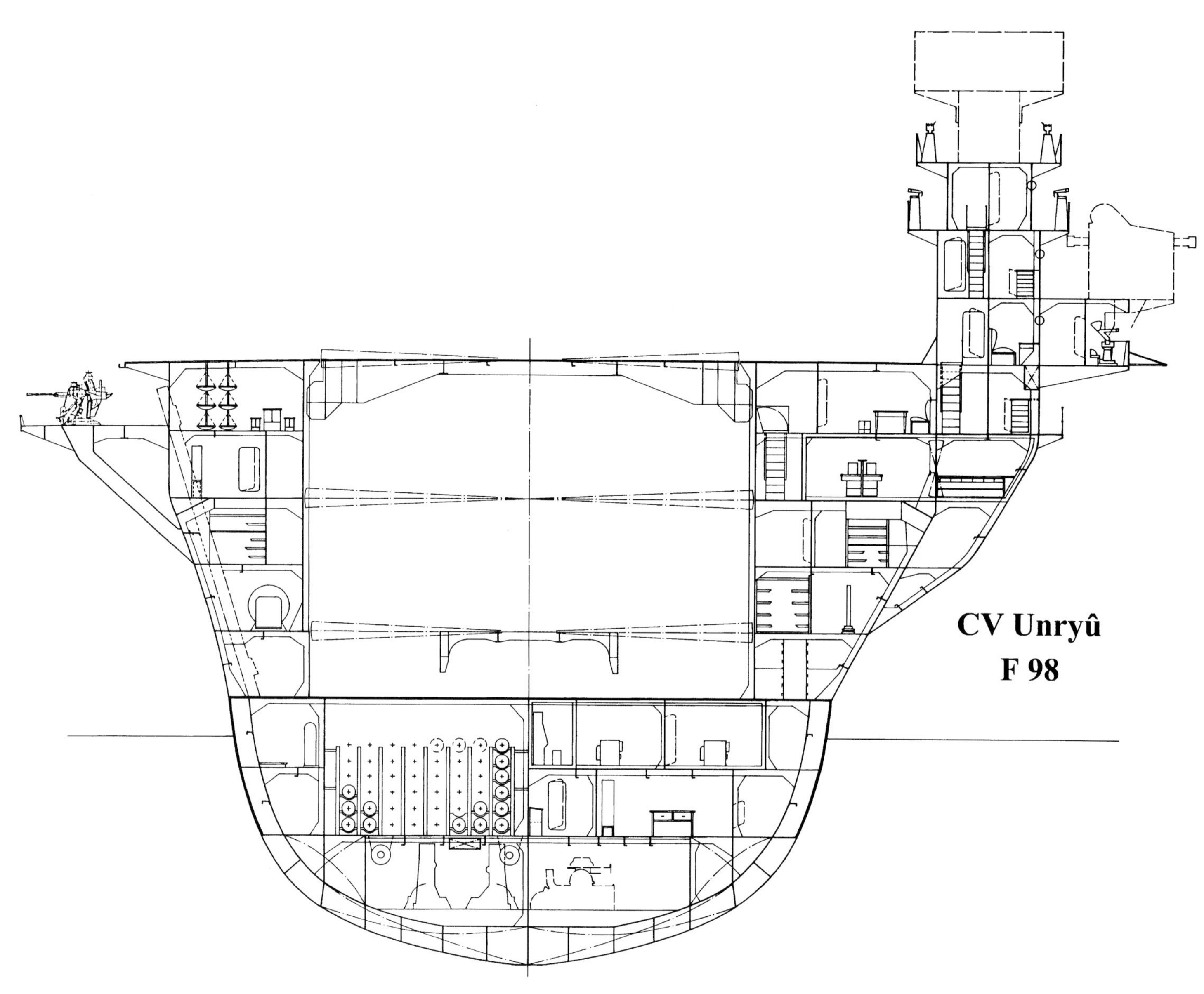

Sections of *Unryū*. Jürg Tischhauser

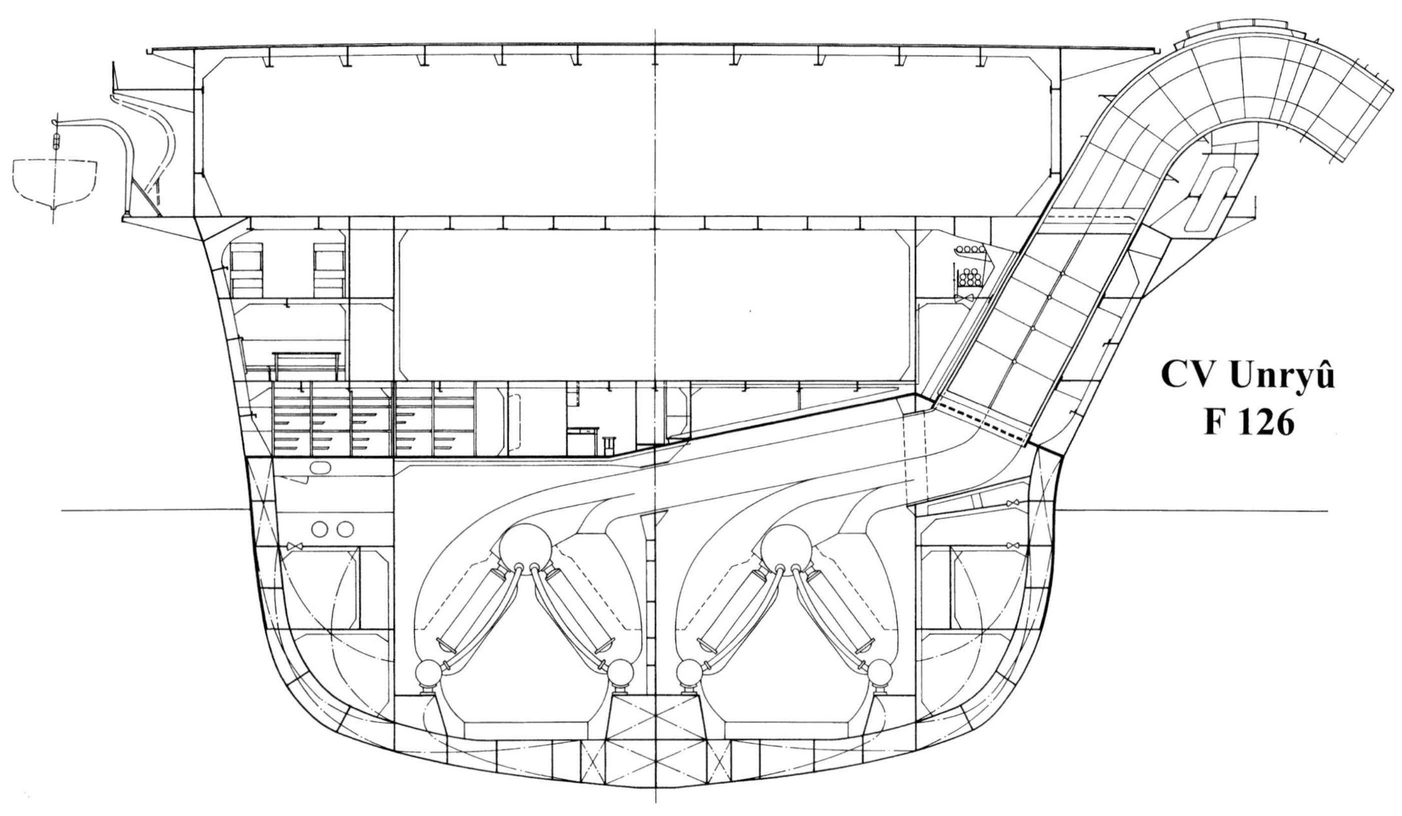

Sections of *Unryū*. *Jürg Tischhauser*

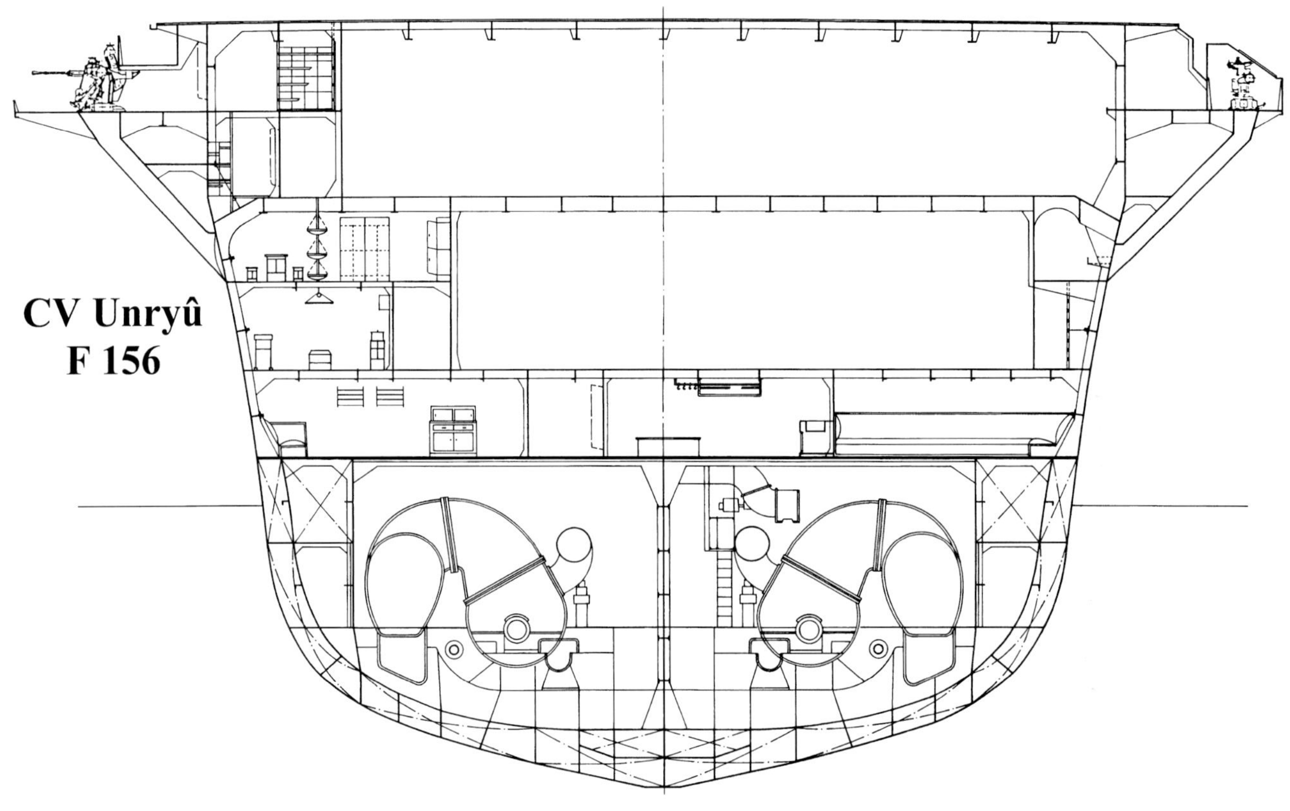

Sections of *Unryū*. *Jürg Tischhauser*

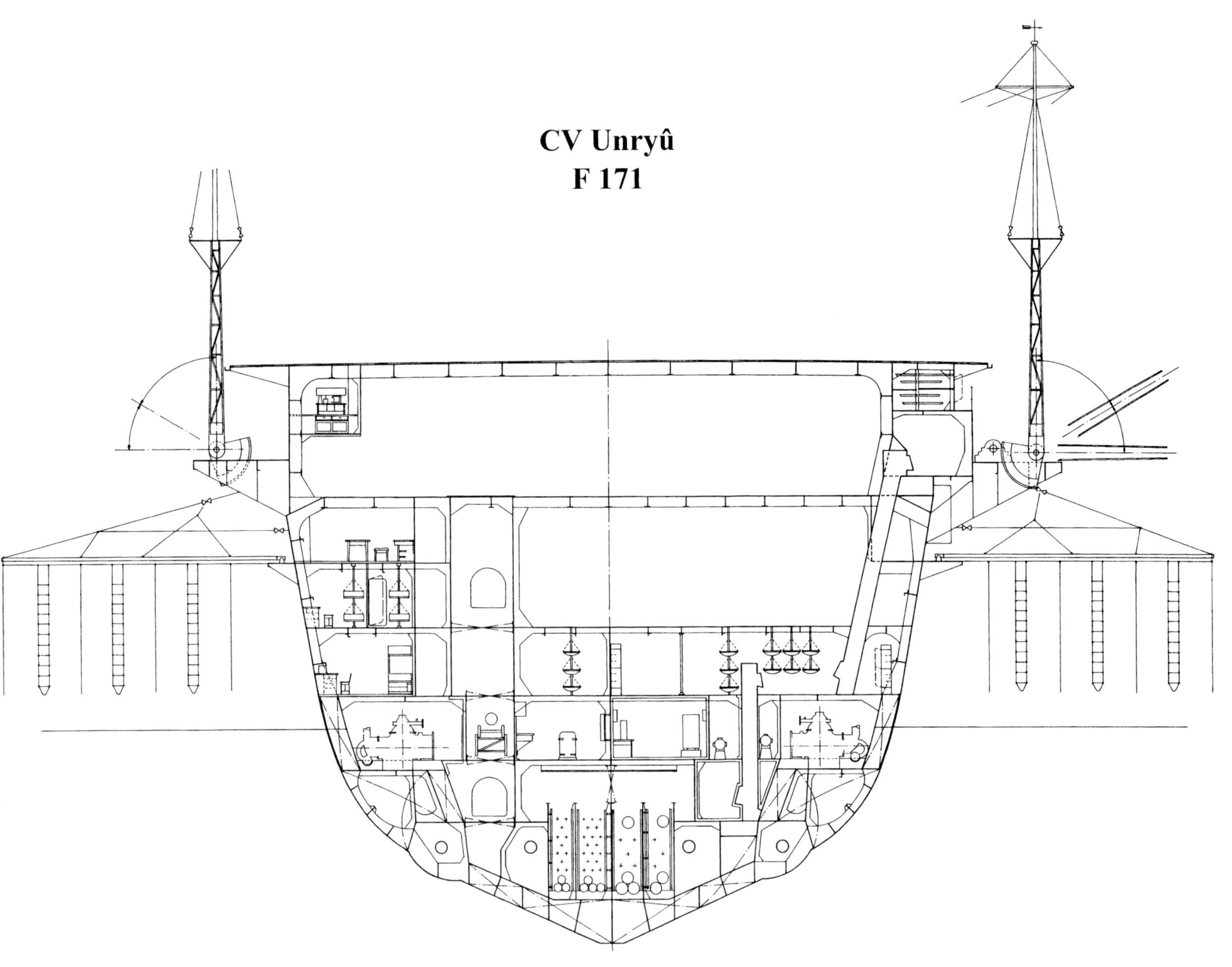

Sections of *Unryū*. *Jürg Tischhauser*

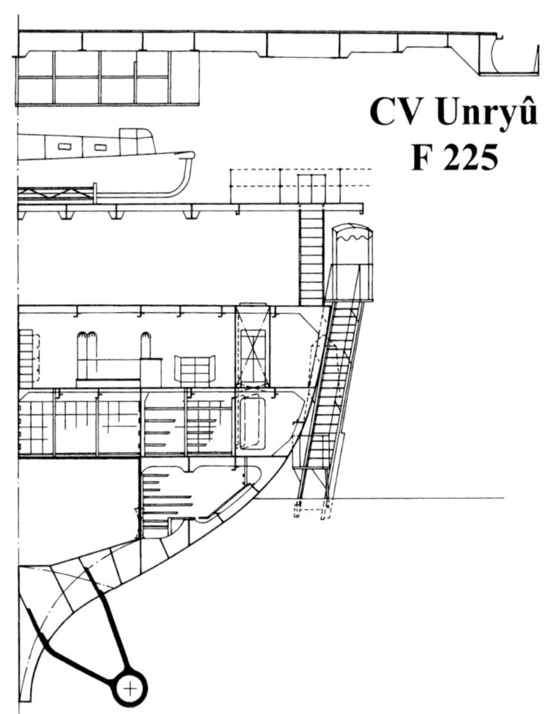

Sōryū's port rudder photographed when the ship was in no. 3 dock at Kure Navy Yard. The rudder is angled 18.5°, and behind it is the port inner propeller shaft.

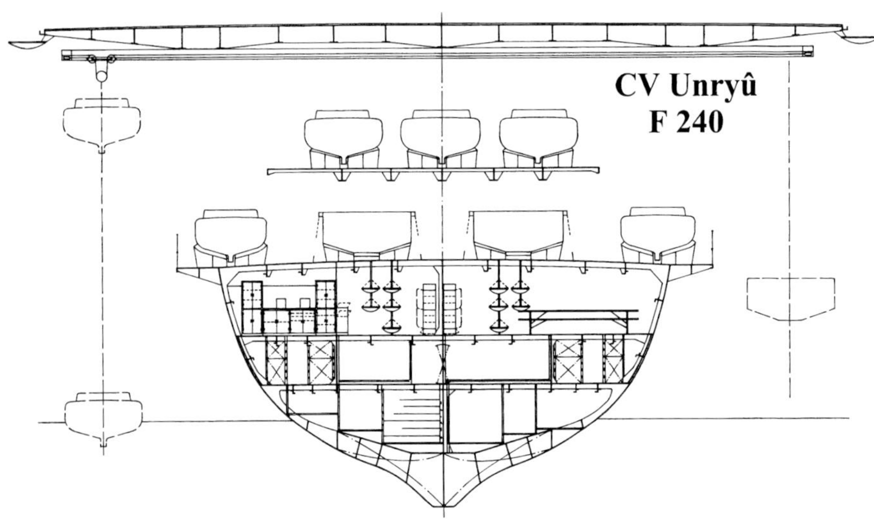

Sections of *Unryū*. *Jürg Tischhauser*

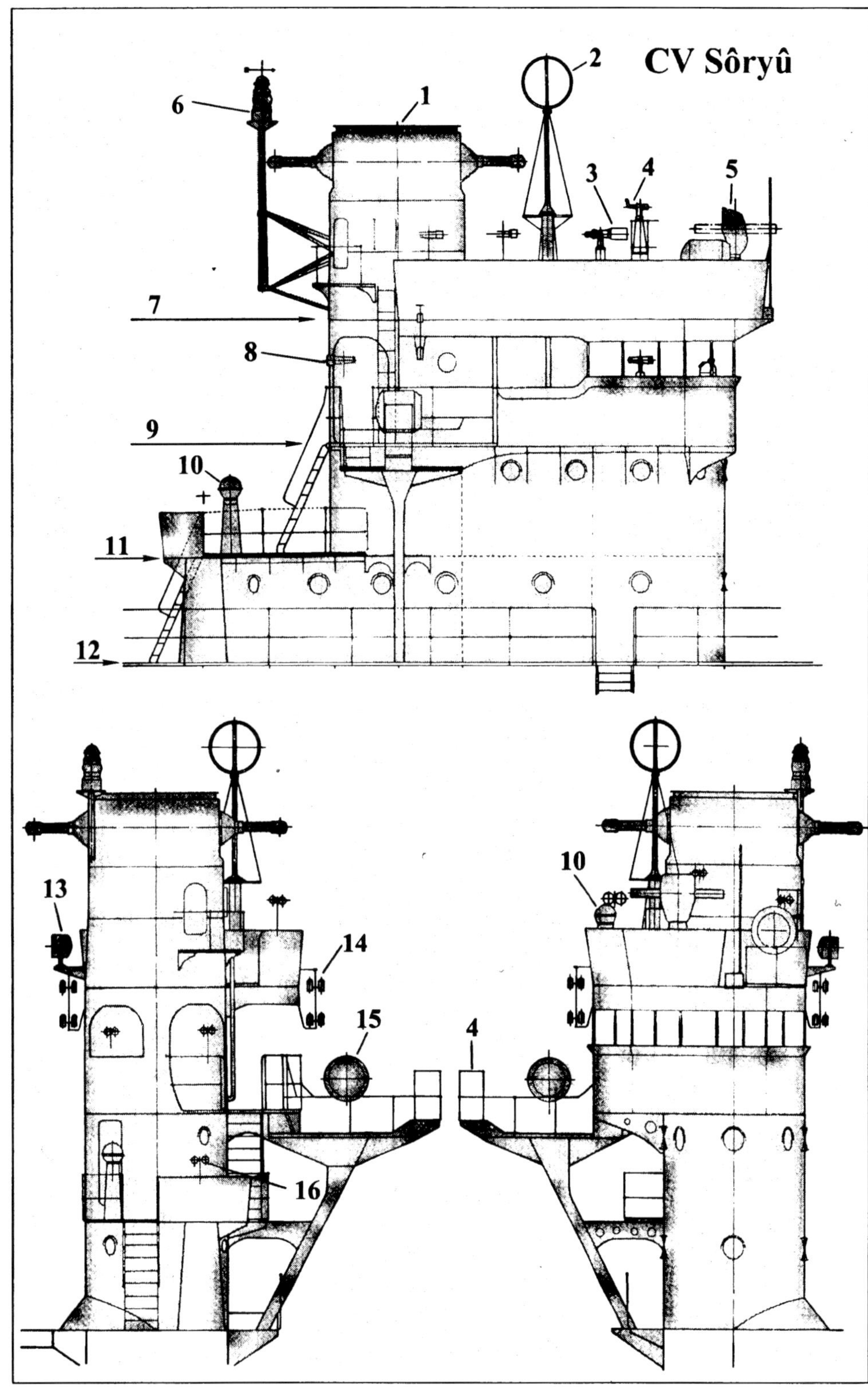

Island structure of *Sōryū*. *Hasegawa Tōichi*

KEY

1. Type 94 high-angle guns fire control system
2. Type 93 no. 1 medium-wave D/F revolving loop antenna
3. 18 cm binoculars
4. Hand flag signal post
5. 1.5 m rangefinder
6. 2 kW signal light
7. Upper bridge deck
8. 12 cm binoculars
9. Compass bridge deck
10. Repeater compass
11. Lower bridge deck
12. Flight deck
13. Floodlight projector
14. Uniform movement signal light
15. 60 cm signal light
16. Searchlight controller and high-angle lookout direction panel

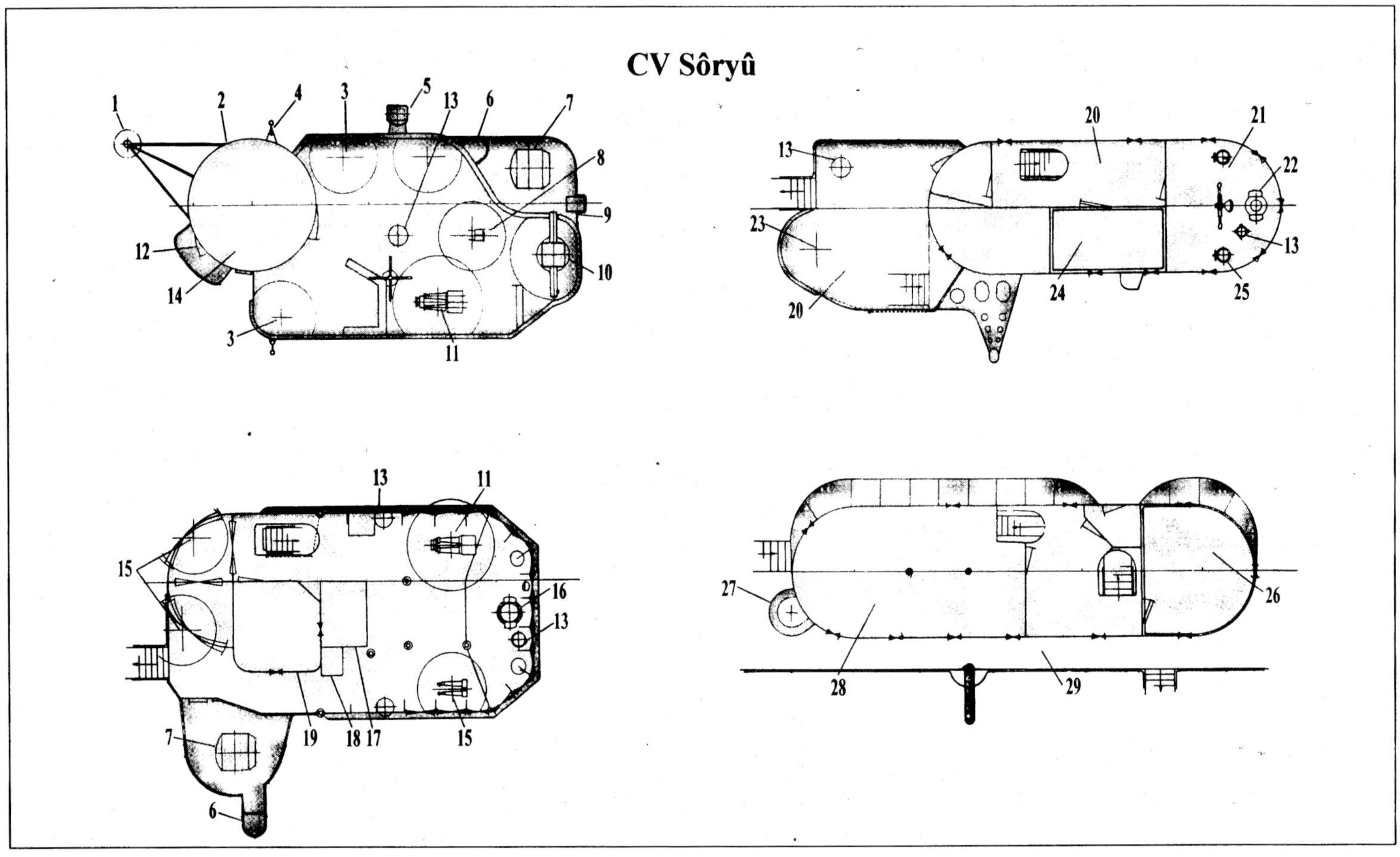

Island structure of *Sōryū. Hasegawa Tōichi*

KEY

1. 2 kW signal light
2. Type 94 high-angle guns fire control system
3. 12 cm binoculars
4. Uniform movement signal light
5. Floodlight projector
6. Hand flag signal post
7. 60 cm signal light
8. 8 cm high-angle binoculars
9. Type 90 wireless antenna
10. 1.5 m rangefinder
11. 18 cm binoculars
12. Entrance to fire control system for high-angle guns
13. Repeater compass
14. (Electric) distribution station
15. 12 cm binoculars
16. Magnetic compass
17. Sea chart box
18. Diary table
19. Information station
20. Control station for takeoff and landing
21. Steering station
22. Magnetic compass
23. Searchlight control and high-angle lookout direction panel
24. No. 1 Goniometer (D/F) room
25. Speed-transmitting instrument
26. Wireless telephone room
27. Support tube
28. Sea chart room and operation room
29. Passage

Island structure of *Sōryū* during trial off Sukumo in November 1937. The island is very compact as a result of the *Tomozuru* Incident. Note the 12.7 cm high-angle gun and the searchlights.

Island structure of *Hiryū*. On the air defense command station are numerous 12 cm binoculars. In the middle on this level is a 1.5 m rangefinder, to port is a direction-finding loop, and at the rear is a 60 cm signal searchlight. On top is a type 94 high-angle director. On the lower bridge level, three of the four type 94 searchlight controllers can be seen. *Manfred Pasch*

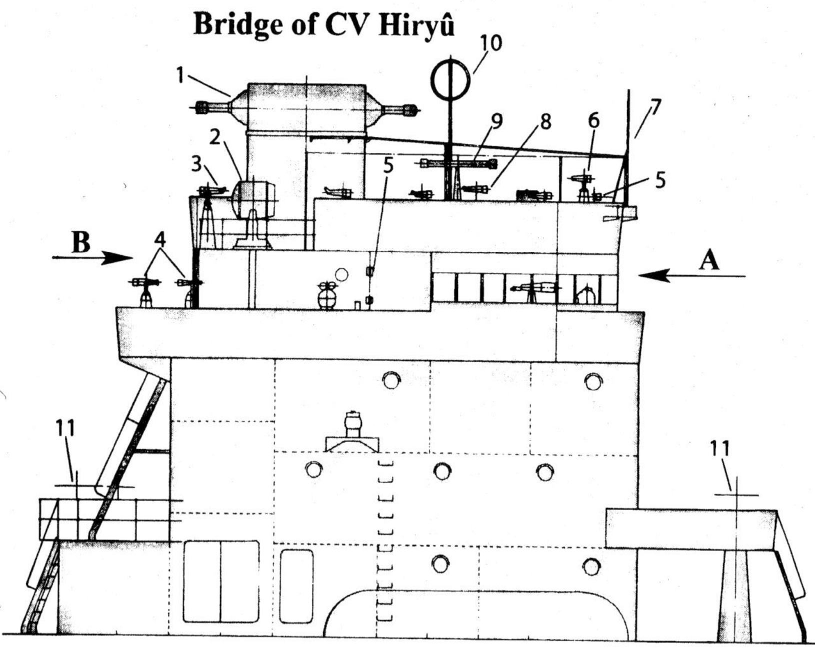

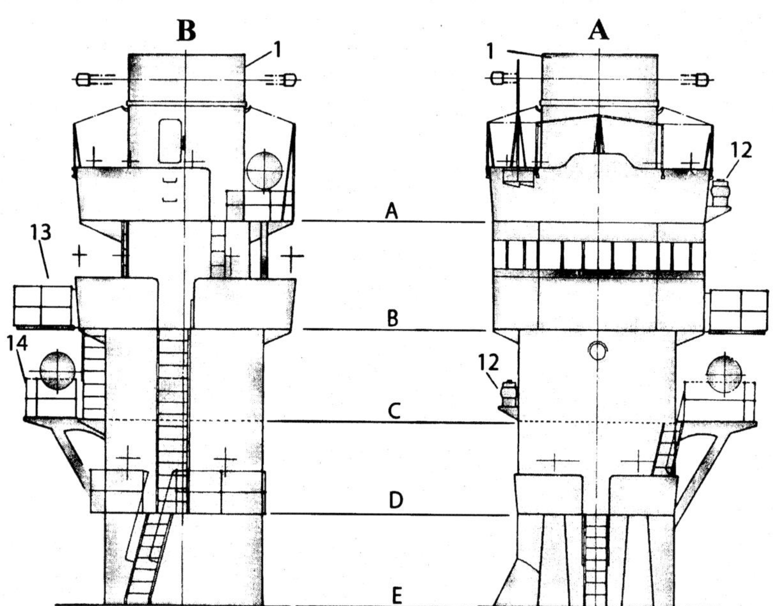

Island structure of *Hiryū*. *Hasegawa Tōichi*

KEY

1. Type 94 high-angle guns fire control system
2. 60 cm signal searchlight
3. 12 cm high-angle binoculars
4. 12 cm binoculars (with Yamakawa light)
5. Turning signal light
6. 12 cm high-angle binoculars, model 12, for chief of direct defense group
7. Type 90 wireless transmitter antenna, modification 4 (ultra-shortwave)
8. 12 cm high-angle binoculars, model 12, for chief of air observation group
9. 1.5 m rangefinder
10. D/F revolving loop aerial
11. Type 94 searchlight controller and air watch direction panel
12. 2 kW signal lamp
13. Flag signal station
14. Handrail
15. 8 cm high-angle binoculars for chief of high-angle fire control system
16. 12 cm high-angle binoculars
17. Cable passage
18. Type 90 wireless transmitter antenna, modification 4 (ultra-shortwave)
19. 18 cm binoculars, model 2
20. Signal flag store room
21. Direction-finding (D/F) receiver
22. Diary table
23. Speed signal lamp
24. Course signal lamp
25. 12 cm binoculars with range and bearing transmitter (compass card)
26. Order transmission station

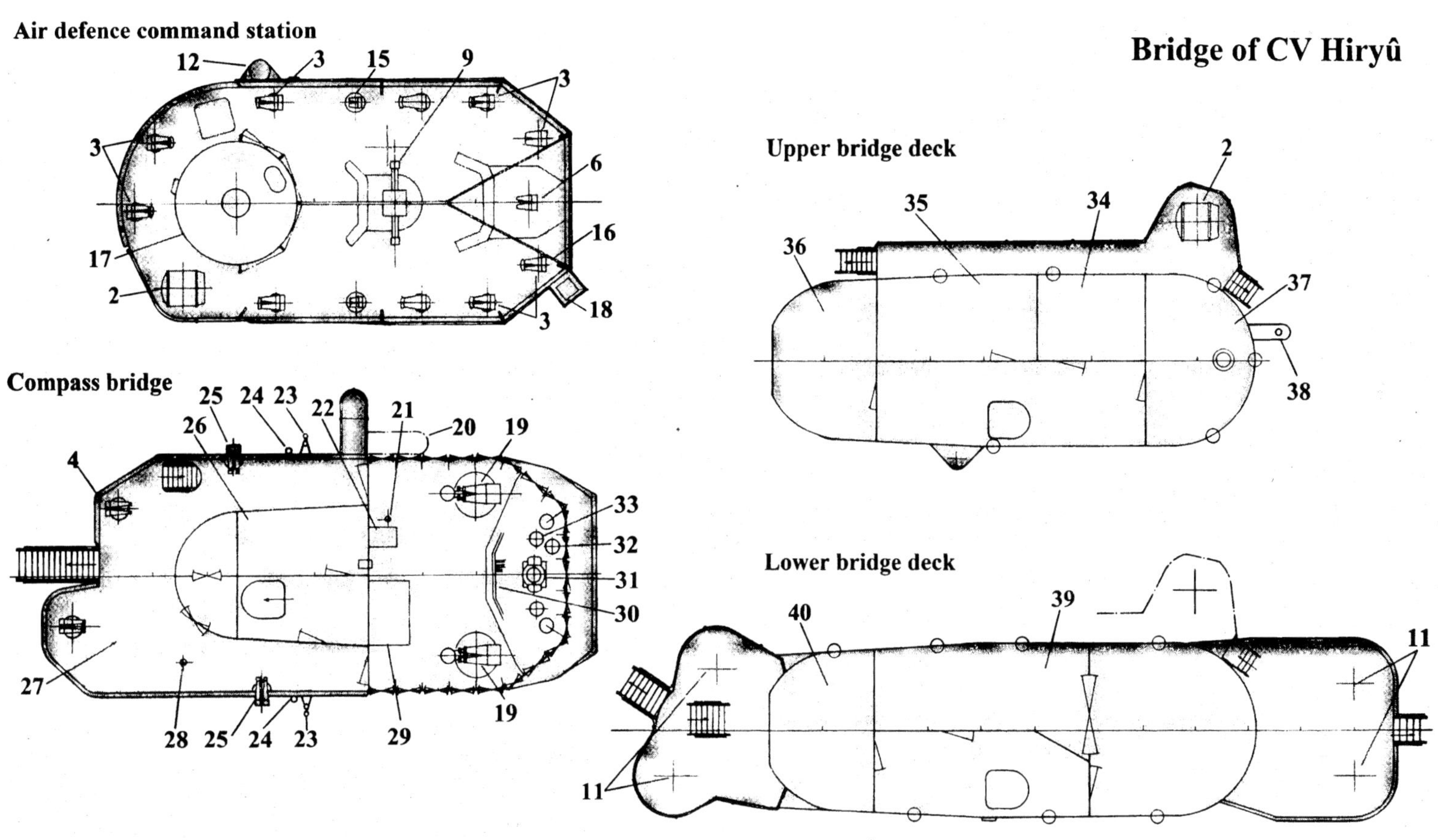

27. Command station for takeoff and landing
28. Support
29. Sea chart table
30. Grating
31. Type 93 magnetic compass
32. Repeater compass for bearing
33. Speed indicator
34. No. 1 D/F room
35. No. 3 wireless telephone room
36. Storeroom for navigation division
37. Steering room
38. Mast lighting
39. Operation and sea chart room
40. Sea chart storeroom

A. Air defense command deck
B. Compass bridge deck
C. Upper bridge deck
D. Lower bridge deck
E. Flight deck

CV Hiryû - Sectional view of starboard bridge profile

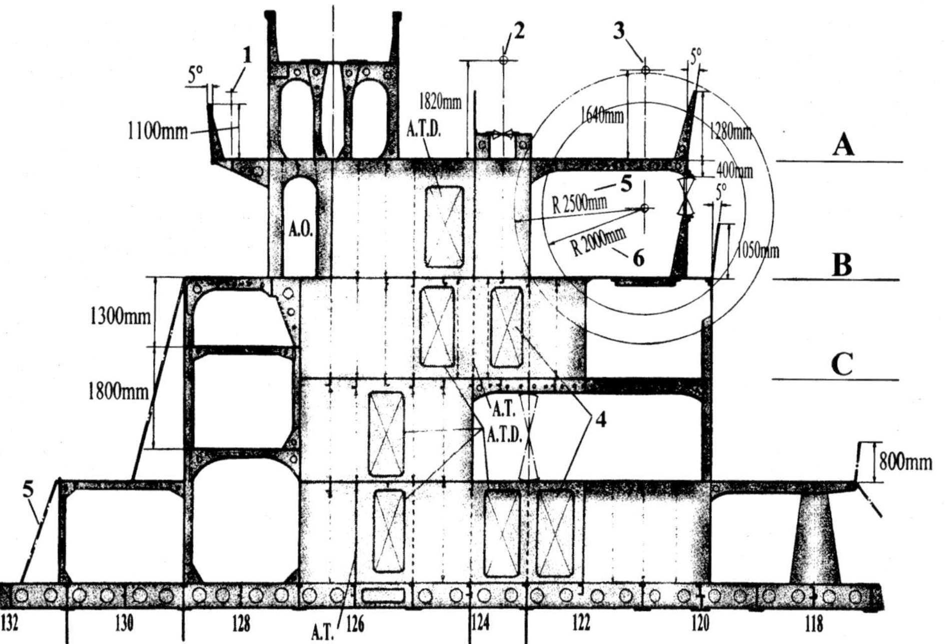

CV Hiryû - Sectional view of port side profile

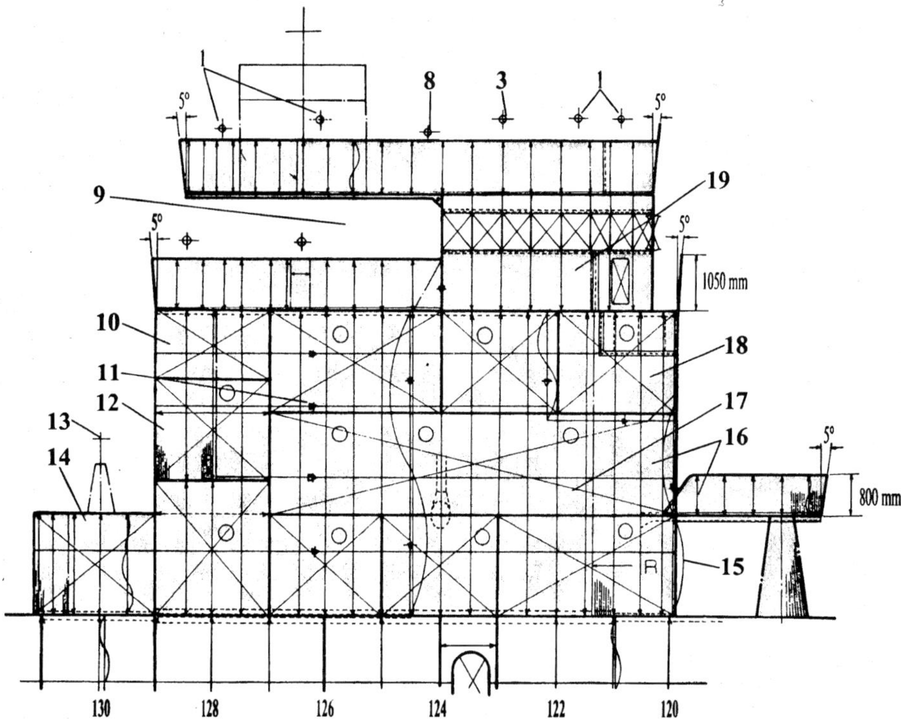

Island structure of *Hiryū*. *Hasegawa Tōichi*

KEY

1. 12 cm high-angle binoculars
2. 1.5 m rangefinder
3. 12 cm high-angle binoculars for chief of air observation group
4. Wastewater-sealing door
5. Magnet field, fixed radius
6. Magnet field, flexible radius
7. Ladder
8. 8 cm binoculars for chief of high-angle fire control system group
9. Command station for takeoff and landing
10. Storeroom for navigation division
11. V-shaped welding seam
12. Sea chart storeroom
13. Type 94 searchlight controller and air watch panel
14. Storeroom for hand flags
15. Welded structure
16. Reinforcement material
17. Operation and sea chart room
18. Steering room
19. Compass bridge

A. Air defense command station
B. Compass bridge
C. Upper bridge

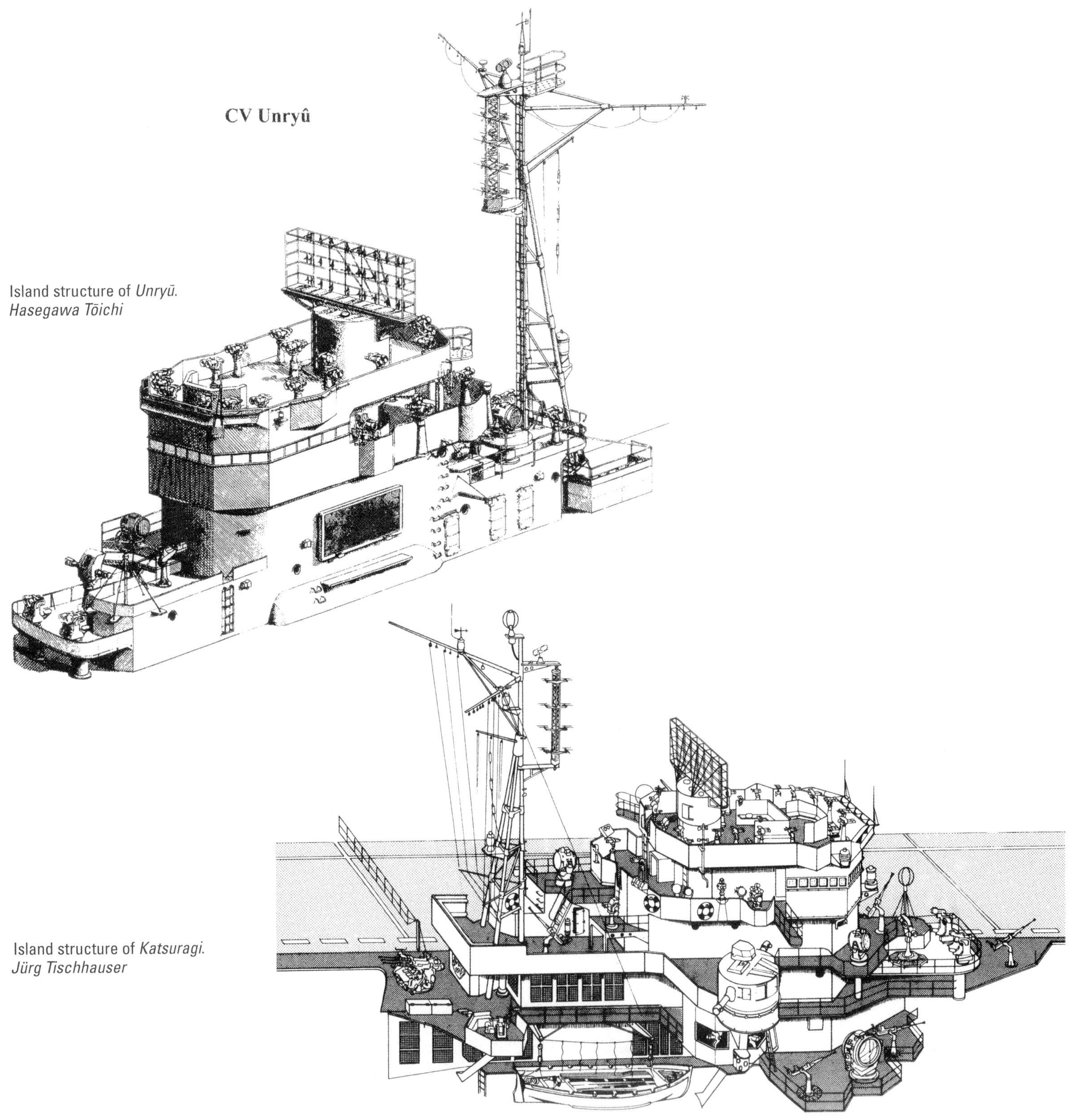

Island structure of *Unryū*.
Hasegawa Tōichi

Island structure of *Katsuragi*.
Jürg Tischhauser

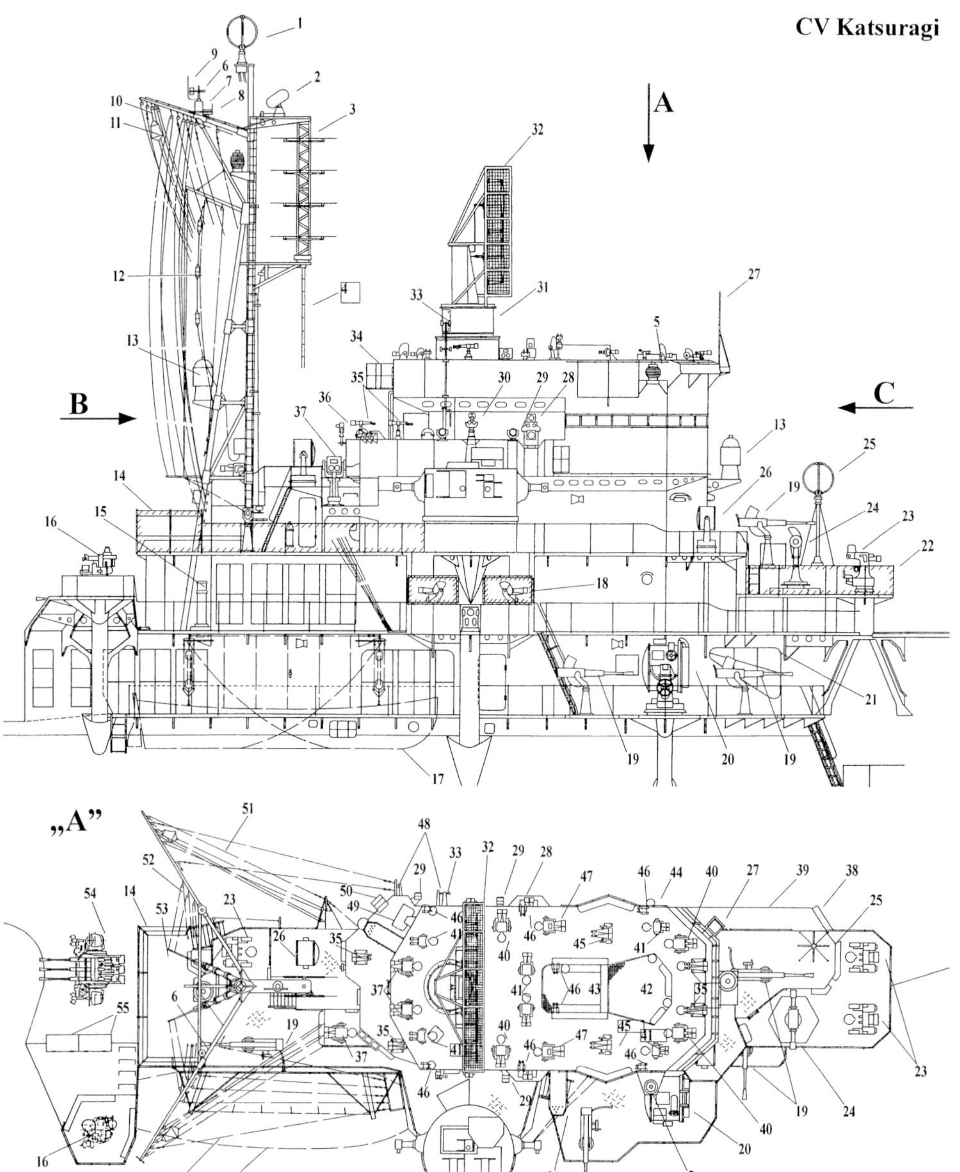

Island structure of *Katsuragi*. *Jürg Tischhauser*

KEY

1. Medium-wave D/F revolving loop aerial
2. Type E-27 counterradar
3. Type 13 radar
4. Cable connection to radar room
5. 2 kW signal lamp, model 1, modification 2 (two positions)
6. Type 92 wind direction transmitter
7. Flashing signal lamp
8. Nondirectional antenna
9. Lightning conductor
10. Mark line
11. Speed indicator
12. Twin signal lamp
13. All-direction signal lamp (two positions)
14. Flag hangar
15. Steam whistle
16. Type 95 machine gun director
17. 9 m lifeboat
18. Type 13 sea surface watch direction panel (two positions)
19. Type 96 25 mm single machine gun (four positions)
20. No. 1 type 96 110 cm searchlight, model 1
21. Boiler room ventilation opening
22. Side screen (canvas)
23. Type 96 searchlight director (controller)
24. Type 96 1.5 m rangefinder on naval pedestal (for navigation)
25. D/F revolving loop antenna
26. 60 cm signal searchlight, model 1 (two positions)
27. Type 90 ultra-shortwave transmitter antenna
28. Type 2 signal and watch panel (two positions)
29. 20 cm signal light, model 1 (four positions)
30. Sea surface watch and searchlight direction officer's 12 cm binoculars (with Yamakawa lamp) (two positions)
31. Radar room
32. Type 21 radar
33. Squadron action signal lamp (two positions)

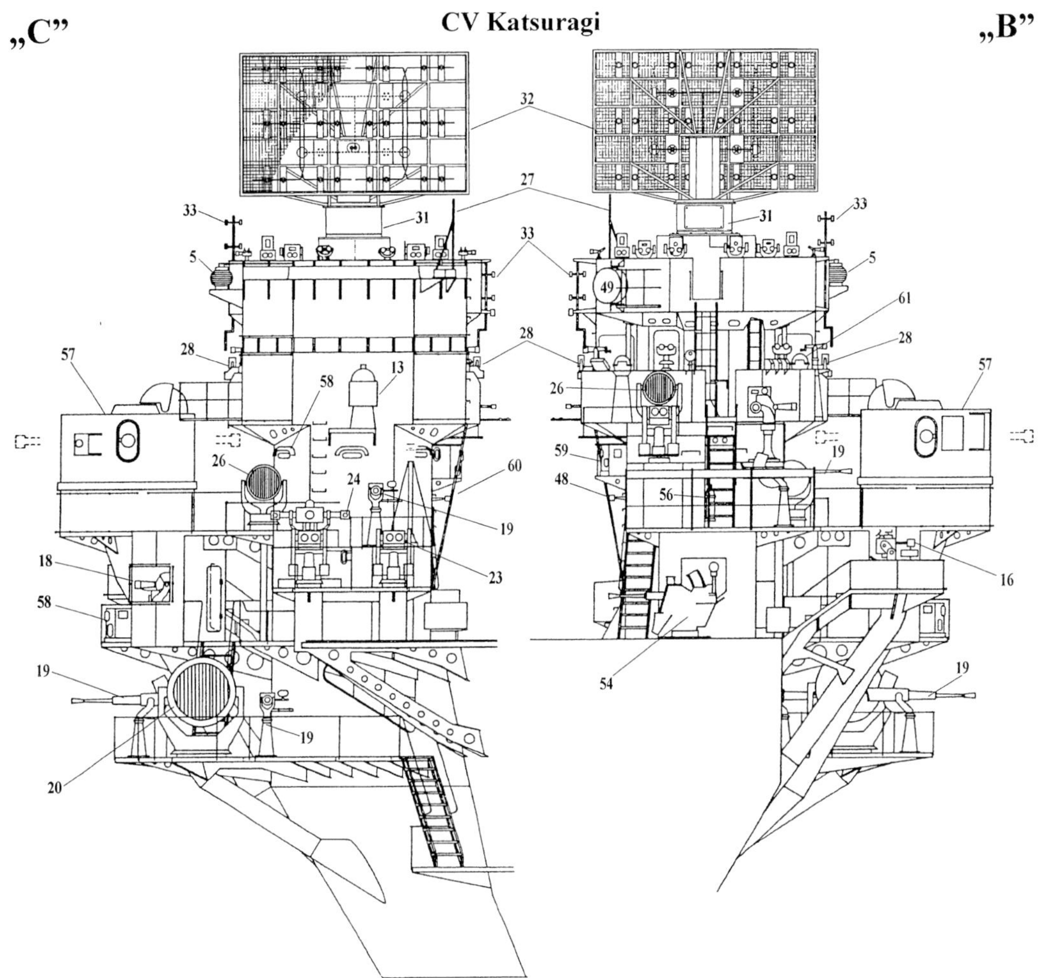

34. Hand flag signal post (two positions)
35. 12 cm binoculars on naval pedestal (ten positions, four on the bridge)
36. Direction signal lamp
37. 12 cm high-angle binoculars (two positions)
38. Gearbox
39. Life jacket box
40. 12 cm high-angle binoculars (seven positions, four on the bridge)
41. 8 cm high-angle binoculars (six positions)
42. Steering-direction post
43. Radar observation direction post for combat air patrol (CAP)
44. Air signal lamp (supposed to be IFF for approaching planes)
45. 12 cm high-angle binoculars for AA officer (two positions)
46. 6 cm high-angle binoculars with range and bearing transmitter (13 positions, eight on the bridge)
47. 12 cm high-angle binoculars (two positions)
48. Bridge signal lamp (three positions)
49. Loudspeaker
50. Wind direction and wind force (speed) receiver box
51. Wireless antenna (two positions)
52. Flag rope (two positions)
53. Signal post
54. Type 96 25 mm machine gun
55. Machine-gun ammunition box
56. Ladder
57. Type 96 high-angle gunfire control system
58. Slit (three positions)
59. General receiver (supposed to be for IFF) (two positions)
60. Vertical ladder to air defense post
61. Bearing (azimuth) compass, Kampon (i.e., Navy Technical Department) type (five positions)

The island of *Katsuragi* was different from the *Unryū*'s. Photo from July 1946. *US National Archives*

Katsuragi's bridge postwar, with the compass, numerous controls and voice pipes, and a pair of large binoculars. *US National Archives*

Katsuragi's bridge. *US Naval Technical Mission to Japan*

CHAPTER 6

Protection

Armor

The medium-sized aircraft carriers had only light protection and thus had to rely heavily on compartmentation. *Sōryū* had a tapered belt of NVNC 140–35 mm, whereas *Hiryū*'s was slightly better, with 140–50 mm. Belt armor in the area of the machinery spaces consisted of 40 mm CNC in both ships. At the magazines, *Hiryū*'s belt armor was 150 mm. Armor over the magazines was 56 mm in both ships. The strength deck was the upper hangar deck, and amidships this consisted of several layers of Dücol steel (DS). *Sōryū*'s middle deck was 40 mm thick, and *Hiryū*'s was 56 mm.

Regarding protection, *Unryū*, *Amagi*, *Kasagi*, and *Ikoma* had virtually the same armor, but *Katsuragi* and *Aso*, built by Kure Navy Yard, differed in a number of respects. The latter two ships had a tapered belt of NVNC with a thickness from 100 mm to 25 mm. The lower platform deck above the magazines had CNC_1 armor 56 mm thick.

The machinery spaces and also the auxiliary machinery rooms were protected by a double layer of 25 mm plates of DS at the sides, of which 1.5 m was above and 3.3 m below the waterline. The bottom from the flat keel out to no. 4 longitudinal was also of double 25 mm DS plating, and this was, as pointed out by the US Naval Technical Mission to Japan in Report S-O1-3, p. 21, "large for a vessel of the displacement of *Katsuragi*." DS was a construction material, but the IJN also used it for protective purposes. Its properties were inferior compared to armor, so DS should strictly be referred to as protective material, not armor. The lower deck above the machinery spaces was of uniform 25 mm plates of CNC_2. Above the aft auxiliary machinery space, the lower platform deck had 42 mm thick CNC_1 armor, and this thickness was increased to 56 mm above the forward space but on the lower deck level.

The upper hangar deck was the strength deck and was built up from the ship's sides to the centerline from three layers of 20/25/25 mm DS, two layers of 20/25 mm DS, and one layer of 14–18 mm DS at the upper side and up to 8 mm DS at the underside of the girders.

The gasoline tank groups were enclosed by two thicknesses of 25 mm DS plates at the bottom and the sides, while the ceiling was of 25 mm thick CNC_2. Compared with the protection of the magazines and considering the potential dangers of munitions and gasoline to the ship, the gasoline tanks were not adequately protected and constituted a serious weakness in the carrier construction philosophy of the IJN. The loss of *Unryū*, which blew up following the detonation of the forward magazine after a torpedo hit, suggests that magazine protection was also inadequate.

The roof, side walls, and bottom of the steering compartment were of 56 mm CNC_1; the transverse bulkheads were protected by a double thickness of 25 mm DS plates.

Fire Protection

Introduction

Compared with other types, the carrier's fire protection measures and firefighting arrangements were of particular importance. The carrier had a very large target area, which represented an attractive target if not even the main target of enemy actions.

A carrier was equipped with large aviation gasoline tanks, enormous aviation gasoline maintenance systems, aircraft and ammunition, such as bombs and torpedoes, and shells for the ship's guns. Moreover, it was unavoidable that large amounts of gasoline vapor accumulated in the aircraft hangars, and this, in combination with the ammunition stored aboard, likely increased the possibility that a fire would break out. If this happened, the carrier was in obvious danger.

Already the first war months showed that a fire aboard usually led to the most-disastrous consequences. No Japanese carrier lost at Midway had damages below the waterline, and their machinery was in working order despite the bomb hits. They sank as a result of the fires raging on the flight deck and in the hangars, and the subsequent fuel explosions and the ammunition detonations. Even when the amount of inflammable material had been removed, a carrier burned violently.

Despite extensive, powerful, and carefully planned firefighting arrangements, these did not live up to the demands that the war set during the first war months, because no other experiences were at hand; fires following hits erupted aboard both American and Japanese carriers.

Initially it was not possible by built-in fire protection and efforts by firefighting equipment to locate a fire early and put it out. The American carriers already had a built-in sprinkler system in their hangars before the war, with nozzles from which a foam solution called Foamite was emitted. Aboard the Japanese carriers, only carbon dioxide (CO_2) was used to fight gasoline fires up until the end of 1942. Only after the Battle of Midway was a usable foam firefighting system developed. The foam solution was based on a soapy-water solution, and from the autumn of 1942 this system was successively introduced aboard the carriers.

Following the Battle of the Philippine Sea, firefighting equipment was further improved, and emergency measures such as improved hangar ventilation, gasoline tank protection by using reinforced concrete, reduction of aviation gasoline stores, introduction of fire-retardant paint, and increased fire protection in the crew spaces were effected.

Subdivision of the Hangars by Fire Protection Curtains and Fire Protection Bulkheads

Japanese carriers, with the sole exception of the *Shinano*, had enclosed hangars. Accordingly, the first measure was to divide the hangars into separate sections by means of fire protection curtains and fire protection bulkheads. The purpose was to locate and contain the fire in order to facilitate the firefighting.

The fire protection curtains consisted of rock wool with asbestos cover on both sides. The fire protection bulkheads consisted of 7 mm thick DS plates covered with asbestos. The bulkheads were installed on suitable places close to dangerous spaces, vertically rolled up on rollers (blind type). The bulkheads were guided in slots supported from the deck above and from the hangar deck, and could be moved across the hangar from one side to the other. This was done simultaneously with the bulkhead on the other side of the hangar, so that they, together, formed a complete bulkhead. By guiding the bulkheads in slots, gasoline was prevented from spreading into adjacent compartments.

As a rule, they were installed close to the elevators and the adjacent compartment, below which there was an aviation gasoline tank group. The arrangement by the elevators isolated the pits and prevented fires from spreading into the hangars. By the protection of the compartments above the aviation gasoline tank groups, the resistance power of these extremely dangerous spaces was enhanced, with the exception of direct bomb hits. The remaining compartments aboard Japanese carriers built during the war were usually separated by lighter fire protection curtains. These curtains were rolled up on deck and could, if need be, be let down with full force. Despite their rather modest effect, these curtains were used since the work done and thereby the working time could be reduced.

The Japanese navy at first had thoughts of using vertically shut roll shutters as fire protection bulkheads, but they instead aimed at horizontally shut bulkheads.

Initially there were considerable problems with the movement of the big sides, and it was necessary to make several changes. Then they could, for example aboard a carrier of the Unryū class, with a 14.7 kW motor close the bulkhead within twenty-five seconds. In emergency situations the bulkhead could be closed and opened manually.

When studying the installation of bulkheads and curtains aboard, say on the *Taihō*, it can easily be seen that the upper hangar deck was subdivided into five fire protection sections, and the lower hangar deck into four such sections. The elevators and each adjacent section (#1 forward, #5 upper, and #4 lower, respectively) were separated by fire protection bulkheads; the others were separated from each other by fire protection curtains. Strictly speaking, it can then be said that since the elevator pits were isolated, the carrier had seven sections on the upper and six sections on the lower hangar deck.

Aboard carriers with three elevators (*Akagi*, *Kaga*, *Sōryū*, *Hiryū*, *Shōkaku*, and *Zuikaku*), also the elevators were isolated with fire protection bulkheads, whereby the hangars were automatically subdivided into six sections. Aboard the Unryū-class carriers, the two elevators and the compartment in between were fitted with fire protection bulkheads. On the upper hangar deck behind the aft elevator was fitted another fire protection curtain.

Both the fire protection bulkheads and the fire protection curtains had to be cooled down during a fire so they would be able to fulfill their purposes for any length of time.

CO_2 Firefighting Arrangements

Because water cannot extinguish gasoline fires, there were CO_2 firefighting systems in the hangars, the aviation gasoline tank groups, the aviation gasoline pumping spaces and the gasoline control room installations with chemical firefighting equipment. This arrangement in principle consisted of CO_2 bottles stowed in the elevator pits, and a command-and-control system whose perforated pipes ran along the underside of the upper hangar deck. Since CO_2 has a greater density than air, it will sink and smother the fire.

Below the elevators there was a blank space, and here an average of 175 CO_2 bottles were stored; each bottle contained 30 kg. They were lined up in groups below one another and were connected by control pipes, and by a control rod they were connected to the remote-control stations, which were located near the entrances to the fire protection compartments, near the navigating bridge, and on some other strategic places. When someone in these firefighting centrals turned the control handle, a valve opened through compressed air to the first group of bottles; hereby the following bottles connected to the control pipes opened one after another and emptied their contents. The carbon dioxide reached the perforated pipe on the deck via a rising main.

One problem was the control of the functions of the command-and-control system. As a rule, the first two bottles were separated from the first group and tested. Another problem was the relatively complicated remote-control rods. Mishaps occurred when valves leaked or self-triggered and CO_2 suddenly discharged into the hangars. In this way the Japanese navy lost quite a number of hangar personnel. The system's greatest drawbacks, however, were first revealed during combat damages.

Modifications Based on Battle Experience and the Adoption of a Foam Firefighting System

The CO_2-blanketing system had proved practically useless in fighting the fires aboard the four carriers at Midway, and in consequence the IJN changed to a foam firefighting system based on that installed in the Germans' *Scharnhorst* (later the carrier *Shinyō*) to control and suppress gasoline fires. After testing systems from August to October 1942, the IJN decided in favor of a piped system feeding foam sprayers fitted in the hangar walls, in lift wells, around the gasoline tank groups, and with hose connections on the flight deck. It was supplied from a main foam pipe and divided into numerous spraying sections, each supplied from a separate feeder and controlled from a firefighting observation station. The foam was generated into the foam spray nozzles by the contact (and hence mixture) of the 2–3% special saltwater/soap solution in seawater in the pipes, by using air. The system was operated by electrically and diesel-driven pumps, each of 200 t/h, with suction from a soap water tank with a capacity of 21 tons.[1]

According to Katsuragi's *Ship's Data Book*, despite the installation of the foam firefighting system, the CO_2-blanketing system was retained in the lower hangar, the gasoline tank groups, and gasoline distribution and control rooms.

Changes to the Air Intake Ducting of the Ventilation System of the Machinery Spaces

Before Midway, the air intake ducts for the engine and boiler rooms were installed on the opposite side to the funnels. This proved to be a serious error, since at Midway, hot air and fire were sucked into these spaces, suffocating the majority of the "black gang" since there were no emergency exits from the machinery spaces. In order to prevent a repetition, the ventilation system aboard the Unryū class was designed such that air could be sucked in from both sides of the ship, and the air intake ducts formed emergency exits through which the machinery personnel could escape. In conjunction with these measures, modifications to the fans and to the layout of the openings in the bulkheads separating the machinery spaces also became necessary. Generally speaking, these departures from previous practice required a considerable amount of redesign, but the effort was considered to be well worth it.

Reinforcement of the Ventilation System of the Hangars

In order to avoid the accumulation of gasoline vapor, which had proved to be a deadly danger, ventilation capacity was doubled in the Unryū class by increasing the number of fans and ducts so that a complete renewal of air could be made eight to twelve times per hour (versus 4–6 times in *Sōryū* and *Hiryū*), both in the hangars and the air spaces surrounding the gasoline tank groups. Faster circulation was preferred for the latter spaces, since in case of the hangars, ventilation could be improved by other means, such as the arrangement of openings in the forward and aft walls of the upper hangar and the mounting of canvas forward of the forward lift to ventilate the hangars via the lift well.

Utilization of Fire-Retardant Paint

Before Midway, oil-based paints were used, and these had contributed both to the intensity and the endurance of the fires aboard the carriers. With this lesson in mind, a special paint was developed whose main ingredients were water and zinc dust. It was used in the hangars, gasoline tank groups, magazines, machinery spaces, crew spaces, passageways, storerooms, and workshops.

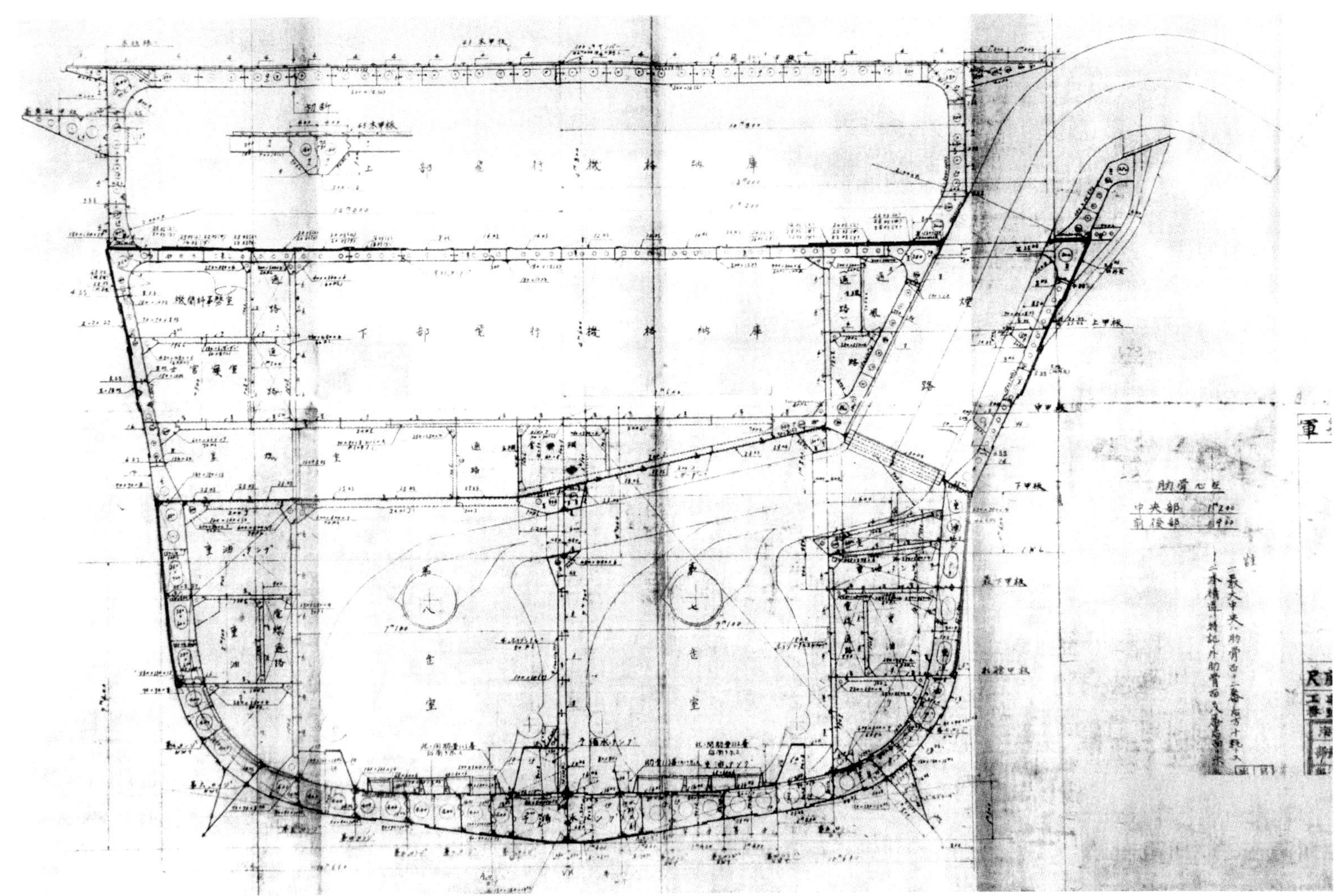

Midship section of *Sōryū*

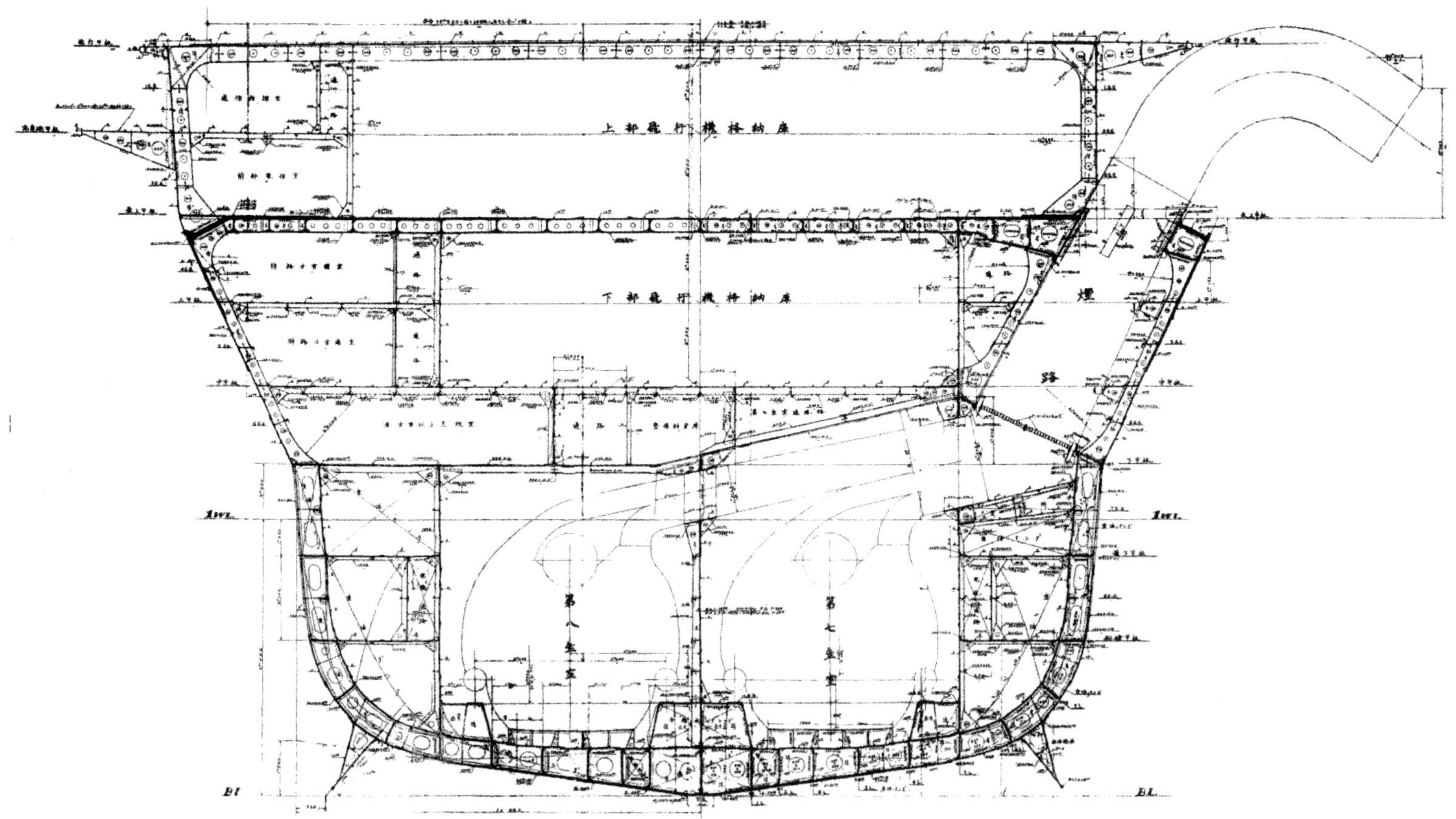

Midship section of *Hiryū*

CHAPTER 7

Armament

Sōryū and *Hiryū*

Sōryū (design G 9) was planned to have 57 + 16 aircraft, in total seventy-three (see table below), and the plans for *Hiryū* (design G 10) were identical. During the Pacific War the aircraft outfit had changed, and old-type planes had been relegated to second-line duties. Consequently, these ships were organized to carry eighteen (+ 3) A6M ("Zero") fighters, eighteen (+ 3) D3A ("Val") dive-bombers, and eighteen (+ 3) B5N ("Kate") torpedo bombers; in total, sixty-three planes. When they went into battle at Midway, they had fifty-four planes each: *Sōryū*, eighteen "Zeros," sixteen "Vals," and eighteen "Kates."

Both *Sōryū* and *Hiryū* were equipped with twelve type 89, 12.7 cm, high-angle guns in twin type A1 mounts. Their distributions can be seen on the drawings. The mount on the starboard side aft of the funnels was gastight and was a type A1, modification 2. Because of their early loss at Midway, their antiaircraft armament was not upgraded, and they retained their original outfit of type 96, 25 mm machine guns. *Sōryū* had twenty-eight guns in fourteen twin mounts (three bow, six port, and five starboard), and *Hiryū* had thirty-one guns in seven triple mounts (five port and two starboard) and five twin mounts (two bow and three starboard).

Fire control for the 12.7 cm guns was by two type 94 systems, one on top of the island and one to port. *Sōryū* was, however, completed with two type 91 directors, but they were soon replaced by type 94. The 25 mm guns were controlled by five type 95 machine gun directors (one bow and two on each side).

For transfer of bombs and torpedoes, there were two bomb hoists and one torpedo hoist. In design G 9, storage of air torpedoes (type 91) was sufficient for the three strikes of the nine torpedo bombers, but reliable information regarding actual bomb and torpedo loads is lacking; they probably did not differ much from the later Unryū-class.

The Unryū-Class

When the Unryūs were first designed, the aircraft complement comprised prewar types as follows:

- twelve (+ 3 reserve) "Zero" fighters
- twenty-seven (+ 3) "Val" dive bombers
- eighteen (+ 2) "Kate" torpedo bombers

Because the volume of the hangars was too small to accommodate this number, eleven planes were to be carried permanently on the flight deck, a practice the IJN did not adopt until 1943. However, as new types of aircraft were developed, plans were modified, and the final air complement was to be as follows:

- eighteen (+ 2) *Reppū* fighters (Allied code name "Sam")
- twenty-seven (+ 0) *Suisei* dive-bombers ("Judy")
- six (+ 0) *Saiun* reconnaissance planes ("Myrt")

This resulted in a total of fifty-one (+ 2) aircraft, of which the "Myrts" were to be carried on the flight deck.

When the ships were commissioned between August and October 1944, the *Reppū* and *Saiun* were not yet in service with the IJN, so *Katsuragi* and the other completed ships were to be temporarily equipped with the following:

- twenty-seven (+ 0) "Zero" fighters
- nine (+ 0) "Judy" dive bombers
- three (+ 0) "Judys" of the reconnaissance version
- nine (+ 0) *Tenzan* torpedo bombers ("Jill")

This resulted in a total of forty-eight (+ 0) aircraft.

However, neither *Amagi* nor *Katsuragi* ever embarked these aircraft types, since the commander in chief of the Combined Fleet had decided that all carrier-based aircraft should operate from land bases.

The bomb and torpedo loads were changed from the initially planned 72 × 800 kg, 240 × 250 kg, 360 × 60 kg, and 144 × 30 kg bombs and 36 torpedoes to the same number of 800 kg bombs but 288 × 250 kg and 456 × 60 kg bombs and 36 torpedoes (type 91, modification 6). Six of the latter could be adjusted at the same time. However, *Katsuragi* was to be equipped with 48 × 800 kg and 48 × 500 kg as well as 96 × 250 kg and 96 × 60 kg bombs. The planned torpedo complement remained unchanged.

To transfer bombs and torpedoes from the magazines, there were two hoists. In contrast to *Hiryū*, the aft hoist was a combined type for bombs and torpedoes, the forward one for bombs only. The aft one brought the munitions up to flight deck level because the aircraft were to be armed only on the flight deck; before Midway, aircraft were usually fueled and armed in the hangars and emerged from the lifts ready for takeoff. An investigation concluded that this was the most important single cause contributing to the loss of three of the four carriers.

The high-angle armament comprised twelve type 89, 12.7 cm, 40-caliber guns in six type Bl twin mountings on sponsons on either side of the ship; as in *Hiryū*, there were two pairs forward of the bridge and one pair close to the stern. To direct fire, only two type 94, high-angle fire control systems were installed, one for each side.

Following the Battle of the Marianas, the close-range antiaircraft armament of *Katsuragi* was substantially reinforced: twenty-two triple 25 mm machine guns and thirty single mountings were to be fitted. The carriers completed in August 1944 (*Unryū* and *Amagi*) had twenty-one triple and twenty-five single mounts. When single mountings were first embarked, no increase in the munitions stowage was planned, but eventually *Katsuragi* was given stowage for 144,000 rounds—1,500 rounds per gun. Munitions were supplied to the guns by nine or ten vertical dredger-type hoists to a position near the mountings; the magazines then had to be transported to the guns and loaded manually. Two or three of the multiple mountings were combined into a group whose fire was directed by a type 95 machine gun director, the standard short-range fire control system of the IJN. For *Katsuragi*, five directors were projected, but it was completed with six.

Unryū, *Amagi*, and *Katsuragi* were equipped with six twenty-eight-tube, 12 cm rocket launchers, of which three, together with their fire control director, were located on a large sponson on either side forward of the bow high-angle grouping. *Unryū* and *Amagi* received their twenty-eight-tube launchers in August 1944, immediately after their completion, while *Katsuragi* was equipped during the last phase of the fitting-out stage. The director was of the same type used for the 25 mm twin and triple machine-gun mountings. There are conflicting data both in the detailed drawings Kure Navy Yard received before fitting-out—these featured twenty-nine-tube launchers, but only twenty-eight-tube and thirty-tube launchers were produced—and those published by Fukui Shizuo, who was at Kure Navy Yard when the launchers were installed. Fukui, in vol. 3 of his *Japanese Naval Vessels Illustrated, 1869–1945* (pp. 199 and 338), states that they were thirty-tube launchers and that four launchers were mounted on each side. In contrast, the official Ship Data Book states that there was a twenty-eight-tube launcher with 140 rockets per launcher and 840 rockets in total, suggesting that six twenty-eight-tube launchers were carried, with five sets of reloads provided for each launcher.

Radar and Radar Countermeasures

According to official data, *Katsuragi* was equipped with two no. 21 (type 2, no. 2, model 1) and two no. 13 (type no. l, model 3) radars. The antennae of the no. 21 were installed atop the island structure and in a recess in the port aft side of the flight deck. Those for the no. 13 radars were located on the tripod signal mast directly abaft the island and the aft radio mast to starboard. Both radar types were for air surveillance.

The antennae for the no. 21 were large mattress types of conventional design. Those installed atop the island belonged to the first type (no. 21) and consisted of two separate transmitting and receiving arrays, each comprising an array six elements wide and two high. The antenna installed on the flight deck was a modified type (no. 21, modification 2) that employed duplexing and had an array four elements wide and three high.

For the no. 13 radar, a ladder-type broadside array comprising four steps and two elements backed by parasitic reflectors was used. It was very compact and considered very efficient. Because it weighed only 110 kg compared to the 840 kg of the no. 21, it was the primary shipborne air surveillance radar of the IJN.

The radar countermeasures (RCM) installation consisted of two radar intercept receivers: one in the metric band (type E-27) and one in the centimetric band (model 3). Three antennae were used with these two receivers. A metox omnidirectional antennae was used in the type E-27 to detect transmissions, and a racquet-type antennae was then used to determine the bearing of the transmission. The model 3 covered wavelengths from 0.80 to 0.03 m (the type E-27, from 0.75 to 4.0 m) and used the type 49 antenna with a parabolic disk 0.45 m in diameter and having a crystal pickup located in the front of the reflector between the antennae elements. This antenna was handheld.

Photos of *Katsuragi* taken in 1945 show the horn antennae of the modified no. 22 (type 2, model 2, modification 4) radar atop the island. This was a surface surveillance and fire control radar, and the only one used by the IJN for shipborne fire control. It was first used in the Battle of Leyte Gulf, and the results are well known. One horn was used for transmission, the other for receiving.

The same photos also show that the large mattress antennae of the no. 21 radar atop the island had been removed (possibly to make room for the horn antennae of the no. 22 radar), and a large Yagi antenna was then fitted and probably was used for air surveillance—on October 26, 1945, *Katsuragi*'s commanding officer, Capt. Miyazaki Toshio, handed over a list of technical data of his ship to the inspecting party of the Air Technical Intelligence Group, which listed three operational air surveillance radars, which the authors suppose to be no. 13, no. 21, and this antenna, which was probably installed for trials of the type 14 land-based, long-range radar.

Sonar and Hydrophones

The antisubmarine warfare (ASW) detection equipment of the Unryū class officially comprised one type 3 sonar and one type 93 hydrophone, but when US representatives inspected *Katsuragi* postwar, they found one type 3, model 1 sonar and two type 0 hydrophones. All instruments were located in the sonar room, mounted on the forward bulkhead, outboard and inboard, respectively.

Rockets	
Item/Launcher	12 cm 28-Tube Rocket Launcher
Length of launcher rails (cm)	150
Length of cradle (cm)	150
Height of cradle (cm)	75
Height of rocket launcher mount (cm)	135
Width of cradle (cm)	85
Firing mechanism	Electrically released firing pin
Rate of fire	28 rockets in 6–10 seconds (theoretical), 16–20 rockets per minute (practical)
Elevation (°)	+5 to +80 (no depression)
Traverse	Complete revolution
Elevating speed loaded/empty (°/s)	~12/~10 (electric), ~12 (manual)
Traverse speed loaded/empty (°/s)	~12/~18 (electric), ~12 (manual)
Maximum range at 30° elevation (m)	~4,200
Maximum height at 80° elevation (m)	~2,300
Total weight with 28 rockets (kg)	2,494
Loading time	~3–5 minutes

Guns		
Item/Gun	**Type 89 12.7 cm HAG**	**Type 96 25 mm MG**
Actual bore (mm)	127	25
Barrel length (m/cal.)	5.080/40	1.500/60
Barrel length o.a. (m)	5.284	2.470
Projectile travel (m)	4.55	1.500
Chamber volume (l)	9.0	?
Gun weight (tons)	3.102	0.043 (barrel)
No. of grooves	36	12
Twist	Uniform 1 in 28 caliber	Uniform 1 in 25.2 caliber
Depth of grooves (mm)	1.30	0.29
Max. pressure (kg/mm²)	25.0	27
Firing rate (rpm)	14	230
Muzzle velocity (m/s)	720	900
Muzzle energy (m-tons)	608	10.3
Barrel life (rounds)	1,000	3,000–15,000
Type of construction	Monobloc, radially expanded	Forged but not strictly monobloc
Manufactured (year)	1931–	1936–
Shell weight (kg)	23.0	0.2432–0.2620
Propellant weight (kg)	4.0	0.102

Gun Mounts				
Item/Mount	**40-Caliber Type 89 12.7 cm Gun**		**Type 96 25 mm**	
			Triple Mount	**Twin Mount**
Mount type	A1	B1	Model 2	Model 2
Elevation (°)	+90/–8	+90/–10	+80/–10	+80/–10
Max. range (m)	14,600	14,600	7,500	7,500
Max. altitude (m)	9,700	9,700	5,500	5,500
Training (°/s)	6/1.5	16	18	18
Elevation (°/s)	12/1.6	16	12	12
Weight (tons)	20.5	?	2.828	2.026
Operation	Electric motors or manual			

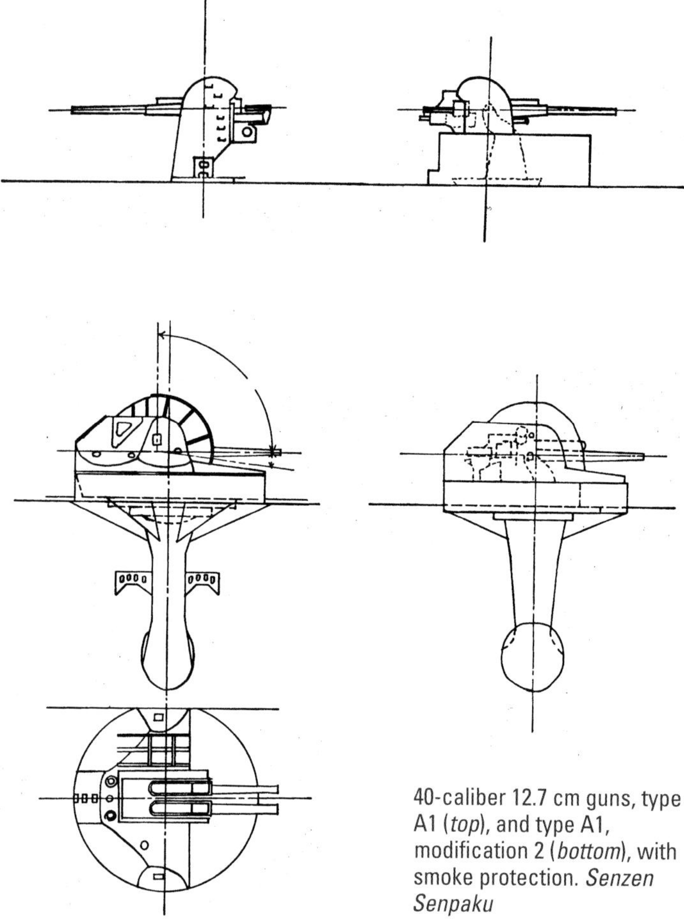

40-caliber 12.7 cm guns, type A1 (*top*), and type A1, modification 2 (*bottom*), with smoke protection. *Senzen Senpaku*

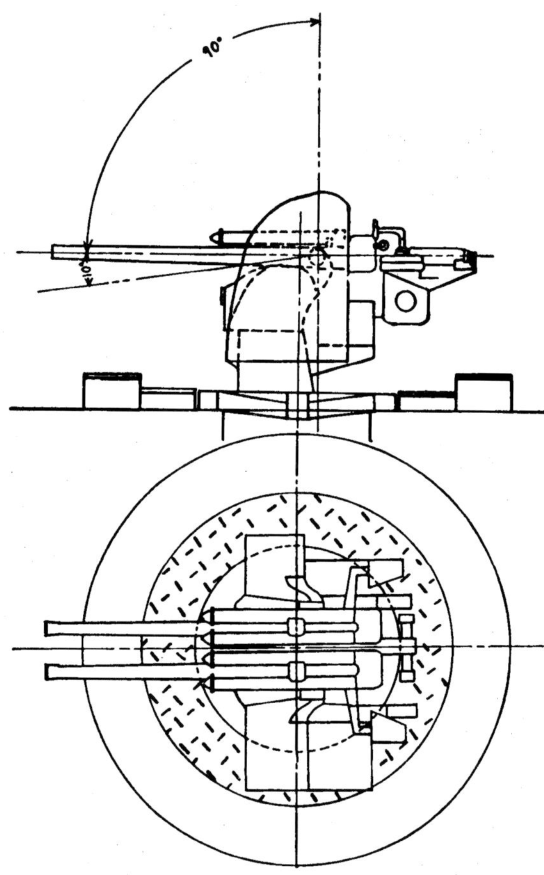

40-caliber 12.7 cm gun, type B1. *Senzen Senpaku*

Type 96 25 mm twin mount on the aircraft carrier *Kaga*

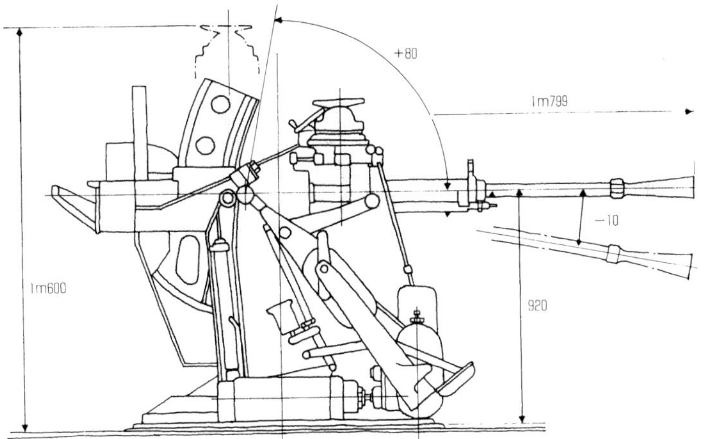

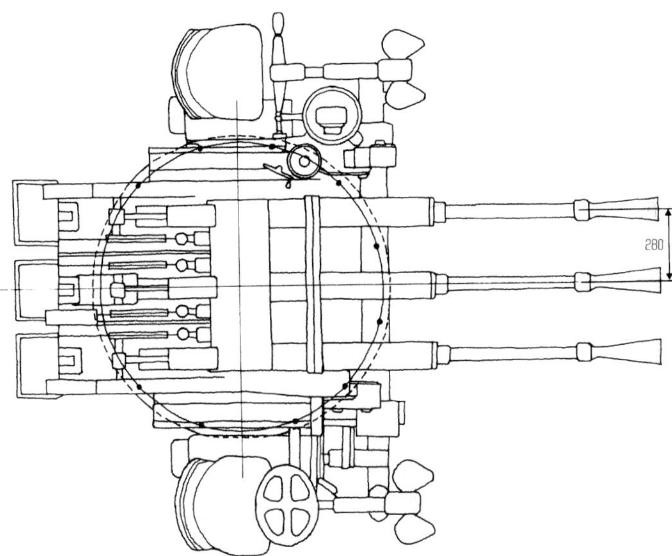

Type 96 25 mm triple mount. *Hasegawa Tōichi*

A Mitsubishi A7M2 *Reppū* ("Sam") at the Misawa base after the war. The propeller has been removed.

Aichi D3A1, model 11 ("Val") dive-bombers

Yokosuka D4Y3, model 33 *Suisei* ("Judy")

Nakajima B6N2, model 12 *Tenzan* ("Jill") attack planes with type 91, modification 3 or 4 torpedoes

Nakajima C6N1 *Saiun* ("Myrt")

Type 91, modification 2 torpedoes aboard *Akagi* in November 1941. In the background are *Hiryū* (*center*) and *Sōryū* (*right*).

CHAPTER 8

Aviation Facilities

General

The determining factor in calculating the strength of the flight deck was a landing load of twice the weight of the plane. Sufficient strength was obtained by a system of traverse and longitudinal girders. The traverse ones were located on every frame of the hull, and the relatively widely spaced longitudinals ran across the traverses to assist in the support. On every other frame, a heavy traverse girder was situated. Since they did not exceed 450 mm in depth, no gallery deck but an "AA gun deck," as the row of sponsons is sometimes called, was installed. This construction required no supports inside the hangars, but on the "overhangs" forward and aft of the upper hangar, where there were no frames to support traverses, heavy vertical support posts were fitted. The aft end of the flight deck had a slight downward curve to facilitate landing.

The flight deck was divided into several sections, which were connected to each other by expansion joints. This construction method was chosen to absorb the always effective stresses causing the alternate bending and compression of the hull by sagging and hogging, as explained earlier. It permitted simplification and a comparatively light construction and was the standard method. Light construction was also advantageous for lowering the CG and avoiding top-heaviness.

Except for small strips along both sides (1 m width) and small areas forward and aft, the flight deck was covered with wooden planks in *Sōryū*, *Hiryū*, and *Unryū*, but other Unryūs had nonskid paint. Planks that were 120–150 mm wide and 45 mm thick were fixed longitudinally. On *Sōryū* the wooden surface stretched from the expansion joint just in front of the forward elevator to the expansion joint situated just in front of the aft elevator, for a length of approximately 118 m. The steel surface of the aft part was covered with a nonskid coating, having the appearance of coarse-grained sandpaper. In the fore part, 200 mm long metal strips were fixed with a distance of 600–650 mm in between at 80° angles to form a nonskid surface.

In order to lead off rainwater, the flight deck had a camber of 100 mm toward the sides of the centerline. Tightness of the deck was at first a considerable problem. VAdm. Niwata Shōzō describes the methods tried in *Akagi*, but when the construction of *Sōryū* started, a solution had been found. While it is certain that carriers with wooden decks had this camber, it is uncertain for carriers using the later-described mixture.

Owing to lack of material (e.g., wood) and the necessity to simplify work in wartime, a special flight deck composition containing a rubber base was developed for steel decks, to get a better hold.

Flight Deck Composition

Vehicle (%)		Pigment (%)	
Latex	60	Portland Cement	26
Casein (5% caustic soda added in solution)	15	Silicon grain	30
Sodium silicate (water solution—Baume 26°)	25	Calcium carbonate	16
		Powdered asbestos	10
		Powdered mica	6
		Fe_3O_4	6
		Weathering prevention	2
		Vulcanizing compound	4

The application was as follows: The pigment was slowly added to the vehicle and stirred constantly until a puttylike consistence was obtained. The flight deck was thoroughly cleaned, care being taken to remove all rust and oil. One coat of zinc metal paint[1] was then applied and allowed to dry for three days. Afterward the first coat of flight deck cover was trolled onto the deck. A second coat, also about 3 mm thick, was applied after two or three days. When the second coat was dry, the deck was finished with a single spraying of light-blue paint. It was important that the application was made in dry weather, since rain might wash away the latex.

Ample securing points existed for aircraft tie-down. These were hemispherical recesses with a bar across the top and embedded to be flush with the deck. They were placed in longitudinal rows with a distance between the rows of usually 1.5 m. This arrangement was repeated in the hangars.

Several cutouts were made along the deck edge to permit the 12.7 cm high-angle guns to fire across the deck at a minimum elevation of about 70°. These recesses had hinged flaps so that they could be bridged for handling aircraft.

On the whole, the aircraft operating area was well planned. However, there were several appurtenances that retracted into the flight deck and were covered by hinged, flush hatches. Notable among them were type 92 and type 96 110 cm searchlights, of which four and two units were fitted on *Sōryū* and *Hiryū* and the Unryūs, respectively. The types of hatches also differed, rotating in the former ships and forward sliding in the Unryūs. The latter were also equipped with type 21 surface search radar, of which the bedspring-type antennae of one unit, together with its mount housing transmitters and receivers, were mounted in a recess like the searchlights and covered by a hatch flush with the flight deck. To starboard aft, about the height of the aft elevator in *Sōryū* and *Hiryū* and farther aft in the Unryūs, was a 4- and 5-ton telescopic-type aircraft crane, respectively, in a recess. The mounting became necessary because the watertightness of the door at the rear hangar side of *Ryūjō* for loading aircraft in the hangar had caused remarkable problems. Consequently, this method was abandoned in *Sōryū* and subsequent carriers and was replaced by a crane to handle aircraft at anchorages, for instance, and to move them to the hangars via the elevators. The operating mechanism was mounted in a compartment below the recess. While 10 and 30 hp motors were used in 4-ton cranes, the performance increased to 12 hp (for turning and erecting/laying down) and 40 hp (for lifting) in cranes with 5-ton capacity.

The large windscreen, installed in a recess flush with the deck, in front of *Sōryū*'s and *Hiryū*'s forward elevator, was still used in *Unryū*, but the #302-class and the modified #302-class ships were or were to have been completed without this device, in order to simplify and accelerate the fitting-out work. It consisted of perforated sheet metal. If the carrier headed into the wind, a very strong wind blew over the deck. Aircraft on deck and maintenance personnel had to be protected against the wind. In these cases the windscreen was erected. The perforation was used to avoid turbulence behind the screen and to guide the airstream over the planes. The screen could be used up to a wind speed of 50 m/s and be erected during a wind speed of 35 m/s within 30 seconds.

At certain positions along the sides of the flight deck, where it was feared that a landing plane could slip over the side, "side nets" were stretched during flight operations. The meshes of these "nets" (500 by 500 mm) formed a barrier from about 2 m above the deck to 4 m and were made of steel wires.

Along the sides of the flight deck, but lower than its level and projecting outside, were standby stations ("pockets") for the aircraft-operating personnel. These stations began aft of the bridge (landing area) and had benches. They permitted prompt access onto the flight deck during flight operations.

Markings and Lights to Assist Landing

The takeoff and landing area of the flight deck was marked by thick white lines, one on the centerline and one on each side about 10 m distant. The landing point was marked by a white circle.

The pilot was not aided by a landing signal officer, and the control during the landing approach was left to his own judgment. This was rather dangerous, but the situation improved when in the autumn of 1932, Lt. Suzuki Shōichi of the Kasumigaura Naval Air Group developed a landing-aid light system, composed of red (stationary shining door = *shōmontō*) and blue lights (vertical movable shining star = *shōseitō*). The lights were fitted on athwartship outriggers on the hull sides, near the aft end of the flight deck and capable of being swung 90° outward. The distance between the two outriggers with different lights was about 10 m. Lt. Suzuki invented a regulation device by which the angle of the connection line of the two lights and the horizon line would result in the adjustment for a proper plane approach angle (4–6°). The pilot checked that the red and blue lights formed a straight line, and by this his plane was in a suitable landing angle. The light intensity showed only aft was 1 kW, and the parallel lines were reflected by parabolic mirrors fitted behind the lights. By the regulation of the light intensity (brightness), this system was used day and night. It contributed much to the simplification and improvement of the landing technique.

Catapults

Hiryū should have been equipped with two catapults, installed on either side on the forward part of the flight deck. Assisted-takeoff gear was desired because plane weight increased, particularly for bombers and torpedo planes, and a longer takeoff run was needed. When in Britain, the US, France, and also Germany, secret developments started for a catapult to be fitted on carriers in the early thirties, the IJN too became interested. Efforts were made to design efficient catapults similar in principle to those fitted on battleships, heavy cruisers, etc.[2] An unsuccessful test unit was tried only once,[3] and the project was abandoned. For acceleration, pneumatic and, for retardation, hydraulic forces were used. Speed was to be 55 knots. The failure was caused by a number of problems, the major difficulties being (1) lack of rigidity in the flight deck due to the expansion joints, (2) excessive weight of 30 tons per unit and the space required by the "Forward Takeoff Equipment for Warships," as it was called, (3) retention of a heavy launching carriage and rail, which would not have been essential for an accelerator, and (4) excessive time required to load an aircraft onto the catapult-launching carriage by means of a crane.

Irrespective of this failure, the installation of one catapult was planned for the Unryūs.

Rocket-Assisted Takeoff

The IJN started the development of Rotog (rocket-assisted takeoff gear) in the summer of 1942, and in 1943, tests with land- and carrier-based "Zeros," "Kates," and "Judys" were successful.

The method of Rotog was to attach two rockets to the sides of the fuselage and in a plane passing through the center of gravity of the aircraft and below the tail to avoid blast effects. The rockets were angled outward and aft for a similar reason.

The propellant was powder stowed in three cordite tubes. With a content of 11 kg of powder, each unit exerted a booster of 700 kg for a period of three seconds. By this method the runway could be reduced by approximately 30 percent.

Rockets were built for "Zeros," "Judys," and "Jills" and would have been used on the Unryūs if they had carried aircraft.

Arrester Gear

Sōryū and *Hiryū* as well as the Unryūs were equipped with nine arrester wires each. The former two were fitted with nine arrester engines of the Kure type, model 4, while the Unryūs are said to have had two type 3, model 10; one type 3, model 11; and one model 12 arresting engines.[4]

Cross-deck pendants (arresting cables or wires) were first made (*Sōryū* and *Hiryū*) from 6 × 37 plow steel with 16 mm diameter and 14.6-ton tensile strength but were later replaced by wires measuring 18 mm in diameter and with a strength of 16 tons, made of the same material (Unryūs). Lubrication was not used.

The wires (or cables) were stretched across the flight deck from aft of the after elevator to forward of the forward elevator. The positions are shown in the figures. Yielding elements of unnecessary large and heavy construction at the extreme edges of the flight deck held them at a height of 370 mm. This height was necessary to get the minimum height of 160 mm at midspan, since no centerline yielding elements were used. Therefore, the tensile strength of the pendants was comparatively high and amounted to 400 kg in the case of an 18 m length and 700 kg in the case of a 25 m length.

To connect deck pendants to purchase cables (which had nineteen strands, 16 mm diameter, and 18-ton tensile strength), swivel fittings, using ball bearings, were used. Each wire was led down over guide pulleys to an arresting-engine compartment situated below the lower-deck hangar level, or, as in the Unryūs, two engines located on the upper hangar level and two on the lower one. An unusual sheaves-and-cable system permitted the attachment of four deck pendants to one arresting engine in the type 3 system, giving an appreciable weight reduction. Two arresting engines were rigged to four wires each and two to two wires each, giving a total of twelve wires. Alternate wires were led to a different engine as a precaution against failure of wires and engine.

Generally speaking, the first two arresting-gear systems used on Japanese carriers were imported: the British longitudinal cable system that was installed on *Hōshō* and *Akagi*, and then the French Fieux system, using cables stretched across the flight deck and a drum brake system to decelerate an aircraft, instead of frictional force as used in the British system. After tests on *Akagi* (resulting in the removal of the ineffective longitudinal cables), it was also installed on *Kaga*. The Fieux system formed the prototype of the first domestic Kayaba system, using hydraulic power to reinforce the braking effect. This system was fitted on *Akagi* and *Ryūjō* before being replaced by the Kure type, of which four models were produced, with the goal of improving cycle efficiency[5] (i.e., to reduce the time necessary for landing aircraft), thereby minimizing the ship's time of increased vulnerability and permit earlier takeoff of another attack force. As stated above, this system was fitted on *Sōryū* and *Hiryū* and also the subsequent newly built carriers. Earlier completed vessels received the system when being modified.

The Kure type was an electromagnetic brake system. In the arresting engine, the two ends of a wire were led to the two sides of a winding drum inside and affixed, to which a squirrel cage was made of rather high-resistance bronze. The drum and squirrel cage rotated against a six-pole stator energized with 120 A at 220 V at the maximum setting. To reset the wire, the current in the stator was reversed. In other words, deck pendant run-out turned a drum of approximately 920 mm in diameter, inside which was a stator that opposed the motion.

The electromagnetic type of arresting engine had a relatively low energy capacity, heat dissipation was rather difficult, and only one deck pendant could be attached to each engine. Taking into consideration the development of aircraft to faster and heavier types, a look at the table showing the principal capabilities of the Kure and type 3 arresting engines explains why the Kure type was dropped early in the Pacific War in favor of type 3, completed in September 1942.

The following description outlines the function of the type 3 arresting gear: When the hook of an aircraft engaged a wire, a system of pulleys caused a ram to be pushed into a hydraulic cylinder, thus forcing oil through a series of restrictions into an air-loaded accumulator. The shape of the restrictions, together with the increased pressure of air in the accumulator as the aircraft was decelerated, resulted in an approximately constant decelerating force being applied to the aircraft until it was brought to stop.

The performance of the arresting engine was controlled by a mechanical varied hydraulic orifice. Six basic orifices were available for preselection. Each varied in orifice size during run-out, ranging from small at the start through large at midrun to small at the end. By this method, the previously stated constant deceleration could be obtained. However, US investigation members after the war pointed out that this system had neither the flexibility nor the cycle efficiency (the foremost goal of developing the type 3 system) of the US Mk. 4 and Mk. 5 systems, and also added that it was difficult to manufacture and maintain liquid-tight.

The arresting-gear operators were enlisted men. Their stations were at, and just below, the flight deck edge and were staggered port and starboard.

Capabilities of the Kure Type and Type 3 Arresting Engines

Item/Type	Kure Type, Model 4	Type 3, Model 10	Type 3, Model 11	Type 3, Model 12
Designers	Nagamine, Hamazaki, Furusato	Chiba, Miyoshi, Ōyama (Sumitomo)	Same as left	Same as left
Development & test manufacture	Kure Navy Yard	Navy First Technical Research Institute & Sumitomo Mechanical Engineering	Same as left	Same as left
Function principle	Electromagnetic braking system	Hydraulic (ram, cylinder, orifices)	Same as left	Same as left
Max. weight of aircraft arrested	4,000 kg	6,000 kg	6,000 kg	6,000 kg
Max. landing speed	30 m/s	40 m/s	30 m/s	35 m/s
Max. retardation	2.0 g	2.5 g	2.5 g	2.5 g
Max. arresting distance	40 m	45 m	25 m	35 m
No. of wires attachable to each unit	1	4	4	4
Time to reset	12 s	7 s	5 s	6 s
Energy source for reset	Electric	Pneumatic	Pneumatic	Pneumatic
Control method	Visual	Visual	Visual	Visual

Notes:

1. Length of stroke was 1,200 mm for type 3.
2. One Kure-type model 4 arrester engine weighed 5 tons; each type 3, models 10, 11, and 12, weighed 6.5 tons. However, *Sōryū* and *Hiryū* needed nine arrester engines, the *Unryūs* only four, which is 45 tons compared with 26 tons. This is the "appreciable weight reduction" stated earlier.

Crash Barriers

Crash barriers had to be developed to realize the idea of a tripartite flight deck. In the middle of the 1930s, this idea was discussed, and the flight deck was to be divided into sectors for landing, preparation, and takeoff and equipped with "special devices" for shortening takeoff and landing intervals.

When aircraft landed, the area from the aft edge of the forward elevator to the stern was planned as the landing area, while the fore part was to be the parking area. In order to avoid crashes between a landing plane and planes parked in front of the landing area, a barrier was placed directly aft of the forward elevator.

Crash barriers were situated aft (*Sōryū* and the Unryūs, two and one, respectively) or abreast the bridge (*Hiryū*, two) and close to the forward end of the flight deck (*Sōryū*, *Hiryū*, and the Unryūs, one). While *Sōryū* and *Hiryū* had two Kūshō-type barriers, the Unryūs had the same number of type 3. Besides the fixed crash barriers, *Sōryū* was fitted with one and *Hiryū* with two transportable types, while in the case of the Unryūs, no transportable barrier was fitted.

The barriers consisted of three wires, the top one being approximately 2 m above the center of the flight deck. The wires were joined into one, which reeved over a sheave at the top of the barrier stanchion. Each stanchion was guyed aft and to the side. The single wire at each end of the barrier was led down its stanchion through suitable fairleads to a separate hydraulic cylinder (or plunger), the principle being the same as outlined for the type 3 arrester engine, but the retardation was much more intensive, and movement (run-out) was much shorter.

The use of elevated leadoff sheaves for barriers was a sound method of keeping the barriers from being run down by an aircraft, although the increased stanchion weight contributed to the rather heavy weight of 4.5 tons for each barrier and its equipment. Barrier stanchions were raised and lowered by compressed air.

The diameter of the wires was originally 14 mm (*Sōryū* and *Hiryū*) but was increased to 16 mm and finally to 18 mm (the Unryūs) in response to the heavier and faster planes, which were to be operated from these ships.

Each barrier was controlled by a single operator, an enlisted man, on the port side, who acted upon a signal from the "landing and takeoff officer" on the island bridge.

Even though the tripartite of the flight deck was not actually realized, the crash barrier and the simplification of the landing by the glide path guide lights, to be described later, contributed much to the reduction of the interval between two landings, 25–40 seconds.

In Report No. 5 of the Air Technical Intelligence Group, dated October 30, 1945, it is stated that crash barriers were eliminated in later aircraft carrier designs because of excessive additional weight required for heavier and faster landings of newer carrier airplanes. Also, barriers were removed from most carriers in service, for the same reason. To offset the admitted safety loss, steps were taken to improve landing technique and arresting-gear and hook features. However, this statement seems doubtful, since even the design of the light aircraft carrier *Ibuki* shows the mounting of crash barriers.

General Arrangement of the Hangars

Most IJN aircraft carriers had two hangars, one above the other. Open hangars had been given up because of the impossibility of making them opaque, keeping out green seas, and avoiding adverse weather influences on the aircraft. On the other hand, aircraft engines could be warmed up in open hangars. This drawback could be offset partly by carrying a number of planes on the flight deck during operations.

The draft instructions stated that the height should be sufficient to change the engines of 4 m high aircraft and also of the three-seat torpedo bomber. This would usually mean two deck heights (i.e., approx. 5 m). However, because of the construction of the decks with sometimes heavy beams, the actual height was somewhat smaller. In the Unryū class the height was 4.6 m in the upper hangar and 4.2 m in the lower one. The upper hangar was usually somewhat wider than the lower.

Both hangars were subdivided by fire protection bulkheads in separate fire protection sections. These bulkheads were steel lamella separation walls, which moved from both sides of the hangar to the centerline, where they were closed mechanically or, in case of failure of the automatic closing mechanism, manually. The walls' recesses in the hangar deck were stipulated not to form a hindrance for taxiing planes. The deck of the hangar had to be as smooth as the flight deck for the same reason.[6] Each bulkhead could be closed and opened separately from a remote position. The fire protection bulkheads were a complicated and work-intensive installation. Therefore, the IJN also used a fire protection curtain with asbestos on both sides that was mounted in rolled-up condition on the ceiling and rapidly unrolled if necessary. Both production and fitting were simplified, and working time was considerably reduced.[7]

The hangars were divided into sections of different length by these bulkheads and curtains. In *Hiryū*, both hangars were divided into three sections, and the length of the forward section was approximately 50 m in the upper hangar and approximately 18 m in the lower hangar. The width amidships was also approximately 18 m.

Since only a few of the carrier-based aircraft had wings that folded completely,[8] considerable ingenuity was required to achieve close stowage in the hangars. It was common practice to stow them slantwise in order to have about two rows (particularly forward and aft). The position of the planes was drawn on the hangar bottom, and when taxied correctly, they were lashed to the deck in the same way as on the flight deck.

The number and distribution of the planes as well as types and models varied depending on the type of operation, war lessons, and the current situation. For medium-sized carriers (*Hiryū* and the Unryū class), the operative number of aircraft was reduced to fifty-one to fifty-seven. Fighters were usually stowed in the upper hangar (middle and forward sections), and they used the forward elevator, the torpedo planes in the lower hangar (after section), and the dive-bombers in both the upper (aft section) and lower hangar (forward section). This resulted in a flexible handling where the fighters were being stowed in the most favorable position for rapid handling.

Even though the draft instructions stipulated that both sides of the hangar should be identical and as straight as possible, this could not always be completely realized, but generally there were no major projections from bulkheads and overheads.

The distance between the stowed planes, including the fuselages and wings of the reserve planes, and the hangar walls was to be a minimum of 0.5 m. In addition, at least before the Pacific War, ropes were stretched between the planes.

If a plane was to be stowed in the hangar for a long time, the forward and aft parts of the fuselage and the wings were to be relieved by supports.

It was intended that during operations, about twelve planes in excess of the number normally embarked should be carried, lashed on the flight deck. In fact there were almost no operations during which this intention was realized.

To embark aircraft in an anchorage, port, base, or bay—when planes could not land on the flight deck due to lack of wind—a large opening closed by a door was cut in the rear wall of the upper hangar. However, this was a rather dangerous method because water could enter the hangar, as experienced in *Ryūjō*. Beginning with *Sōryū*, only a 2 × 2 m opening and a strong, watertight door were fitted.

On the hangar walls and on the ceiling, spare parts for aircraft (propellers, reserve tanks, machine gun carriages, bombsights, bomb release fittings, etc.) were fixed. There were also various types of hoses and large portable lamps. As addition to lighting on the ceiling and the portable lamps, small, swiveling searchlights were installed on the upper part of the hangar walls, because good working light was important. There were particular stipulations regarding electric cables in the hangars.

Overhead traveling hoists on I beams with turntables and branch lines were installed for aircraft engine transfer and torpedoes. Actual change of engines was not executed with the hoists, but a ringlike fitting, also fitted on the ceiling, was used. It was therefore not necessary that the hoists/pulleys could reach the whole hangar area.

The CO_2 and foam firefighting systems are described elsewhere. The stipulation to fit extinguishing water tanks[9] in the various fire protection sections was largely ignored, at least until June 1944, because of the low efficiency. The tanks also obstructed the free taxiing of planes in the hangar.

Steam pipes for heating were placed in the hangars to avoid too-low temperatures.

Elevator trunks extended entirely through both hangars, making it impossible to move planes from one bay to the next without lowering the elevator platform to bridge the gap. For the lower hangar level, portable gangways were provided to bridge the elevator pits. Around the elevator trunks, a 1 m high coaming was fitted on the hangar deck to prevent the leaking of avgas vapor. Hatches offering access to the hangars were likewise secured.

Aircraft Engine Examination Shop

In the medium-sized carriers, spare engines were stored on the platform deck, while the engine examination shop was situated to port at the aft end of the upper hangar. Both compartments were connected by a large hatch in the examination shop, trunked down to the spare engine room. An overhead traveling hoist was used for lifting spare engines from the store, landing defective engines, and shipping replacements. The capacity for spare engines was approximately one-third of the plane complement: thus, eighteen engines on *Hiryū*.

In the latter half of the Pacific War, repair of faulty aircraft engines was given up, mainly due to a lack of skilled mechanics. Instead the general tendency was to keep damaged planes, or those with faulty engines, in reserve and to land them on return to base, where they could be repaired and serviced.

The Unryūs never received their planned aircraft complement, and the question of how to handle faulty engines was theoretical only. This was because the commander in chief of the Combined Fleet had decided in early October 1944 that carrier-based aircraft should operate from land bases.

Aviation Gasoline Supply Systems

General

The avgas tanks constitute the greatest fire hazard aboard an aircraft carrier. However, the IJN did not sufficiently recognize this danger at the beginning of the development of this ship type, and even later, when a naval architect required the shift of the avgas tank groups to within the main protection zone, the arrangement of the avgas tank groups outside this zone was maintained. The only reaction was the improvement of fire protection measures.

When gasoline pours out due to damaged tanks, vapors are formed. The vapor spreads, and because it is heavier than air, it spreads deep in the ship. Mixed with air (3–6%), an explosive vapor is formed that can easily be ignited. There are examples in the US Navy as well as in the Japanese navy of carriers that were destroyed by gasoline vapor explosions: USS *Lexington* in May 1942, and *Taihō* in June 1944. *Wasp* was torpedoed in September 1942, and gasoline from open gasoline pipes ignited. The fire could not be extinguished, as was the case with the *Akagi*, *Kaga*, *Sōryū*, and *Hiryū* at Midway.

From these examples, it was clear that measures must embrace the following:

- the inflammability of aviation gasoline
- the danger of explosion from gasoline vapor
- the design of the aviation gasoline tanks and the gasoline supply pipes
- fire protection measures

Regarding the location of the avgas tanks, the IJN had come to the conclusion that, if possible, they should be located so that they were shielded by the protection that enclosed the magazines forward and aft. This decision, which later proved erroneous, was based on the view that bombs and antiaircraft ammunition should have the best protection.

Protection of the Avgas Tank Groups

Until 1944, the empty spaces directly surrounding the tank groups were filled with an inert gas (CO_2). This ventilation system was exclusively for the avgas tank groups and the avgas pump rooms. Preparations had been made to fill the empty spaces in the tanks above the gasoline/benzene, the pump rooms, and the ventilator and working rooms with the same gas. In addition, the avgas tank groups were protected by mostly thin armor, which could not be penetrated by 12.7 cm shells. Because this protection was quite insufficient against torpedo hits, the empty spaces surrounding the avgas tank groups were to be flooded with seawater shortly before an engagement, to prevent fires in case of damage. Flooding was to occur within thirty minutes; drainage was planned by drainage pipes.

However, all these measures proved to be insufficient, and after the sinking of the carrier *Taihō* the empty spaces around the avgas tank groups were to be filled by iron concrete. However, the double bottom could not be included in this system because the concrete would rest directly on the outer shell. Therefore, this space was left as it was, and only the spaces above were filled. Above the ceiling of the tanks was the protective deck, and the filling with iron concrete was very difficult. To prevent the concrete from breaking, a 1 m thick layer of iron concrete was put above. Because avgas vapor could penetrate concrete, the adjacent rooms were so isolated that there was no connection with the other compartments. Equipment in these compartments, such as ventilators and their ducts, was removed.

Bomb and Torpedo Magazines, Torpedo Adjustment Room

Bombs and torpedoes were stowed in separate magazines within the protected vital part in the hold. Their imminent danger was well understood, and they were better protected than the avgas tank groups. The bomb magazines were located forward of the boiler rooms and aft of the engine rooms. The torpedo magazine bordered on the aft bomb magazine. This arrangement had already been stipulated in the 1933 draft regulations and permitted the use of a combined bomb and torpedo hoist aft, while forward a smaller bomb hoist was sufficient to serve the lower hangar.[10] The load capacity of the hoists was calculated for two torpedoes with warheads or two 1,000 kg bombs.[11] The construction was identical to that of the aircraft elevators.

Bombs and torpedoes were lifted from their stowage bins onto light trolleys by chain blocks (later replaced by hydraulic hoists), and the trolleys were wheeled out onto the hoist platform, raised about 1 m above deck level. This height was necessary because a coaming of this depth was worked around the hoists to prevent avgas vapor from pouring into the magazines. Hoists, fitted above the raised platform, enabled the load (either bombs or torpedoes) to be lifted onto special dollies, which were used for transport in the hangars or from the upper hangar to the flight deck by means of the aft aircraft elevator.

Two different types of dollies were used: one for bombs up to 250 kg and one for 500 kg bombs and above and for torpedoes. Both types were manually handled.

Arming of planes was mainly in the hangars, and fully fueled and armed planes were transported to the flight deck for takeoff. But after Midway, aircraft were to be fueled and armed on the flight deck, and in such carriers as the Unryū class, the aft combined hoist reached the flight deck level.

The magazines could be flooded completely within twenty minutes. In *Katsuragi*, a firefighting and a bilge pump suctioned from a tank in the inner bottom. The sea valves for the flooding of the magazines were within the same tank and had remotely controlled slides. Between the slides was a pipe connection that permitted flooding the tank, and a second slide in the magazine flood line prevented the magazine from flooding. With the slide for the sea valve open, the inner bottom tank, which was a sort of drainage tank, could be flooded to provide suction for the fire pump. However, this arrangement had the great disadvantage that the wrong slide and valve could easily be opened and consequently flood the magazine inadvertently.

All magazines were fitted with a temperature regulator system (manual) and a temperature alarm system (automatic). The object was to ascertain the temperature inside each magazine at any time. If temperature rose to near the critical point, the second system sounded an alarm and the cooling system for the magazine spaces could be started manually.

Before the torpedoes could be used for operation, they had to be adjusted—that is, warhead[12] fitted, depth adjusted, and air chamber filled. This was carried out in the torpedo adjustment room, which was situated in the vicinity of the hangar to facilitate transfer between these compartments. Area and equipment were determined by the number of torpedo bombers. Generally, nine torpedoes should be adjusted in common for one-third of the embarked bombers. Chain blocks were fitted to the ceiling. The arrangement of the planes in the hangar took into consideration the transfer of torpedoes from the adjustment room; a small passage from the entry of this room was maintained.

Mitsubishi A6M2, model 21 ("Zeke") fighters are prepared to take off from *Shōkaku* during the Battle of Santa Cruz Islands on October 26, 1942.

A type 92 carrier attack aircraft takes off as seen from the bridge of *Sōryū*.

Sōryū during trials off Saiki Bay in December 1937. A plane has just touched down and note that the wooden part of the flight deck is placed fore-and-aft and not athwartships as in *Ryūjō*. The expansion joints in the deck can be seen

Flight operations during *Sōryū*'s trials off Saiki Bay in December 1937. A type 92 carrier attack aircraft is about to land. Note the white circle, the white centerline, the smoke generated to show the wind direction, and the arresting cables.

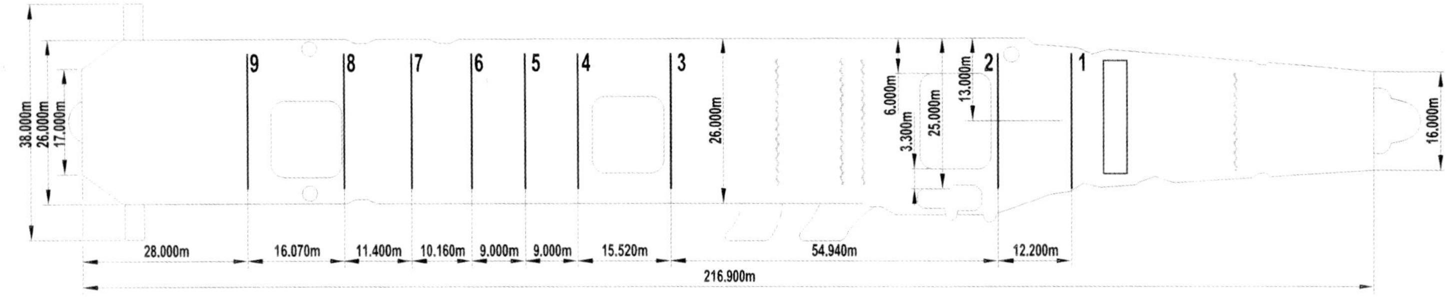

Flight deck of *Sōryū*. *Waldemar Trojca*

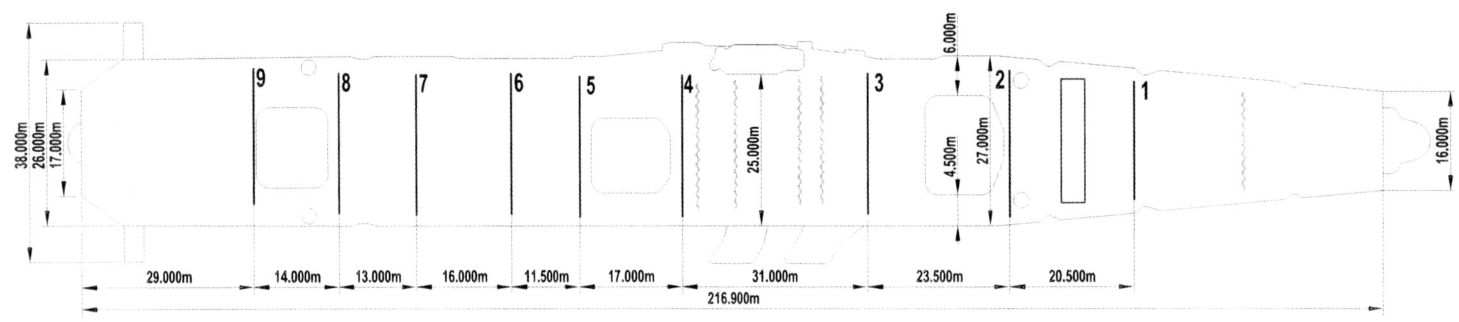

Flight deck of *Hiryū*. *Waldemar Trojca*

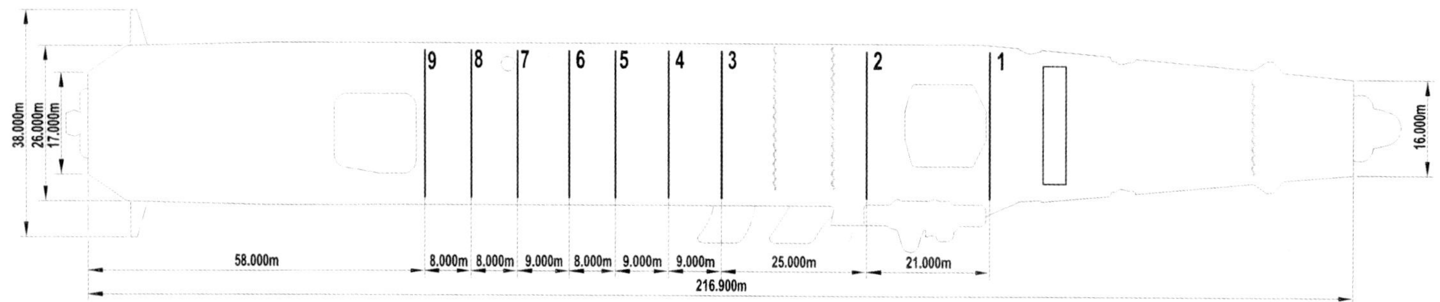

Flight deck of *Unryū*. *Waldemar Trojca*

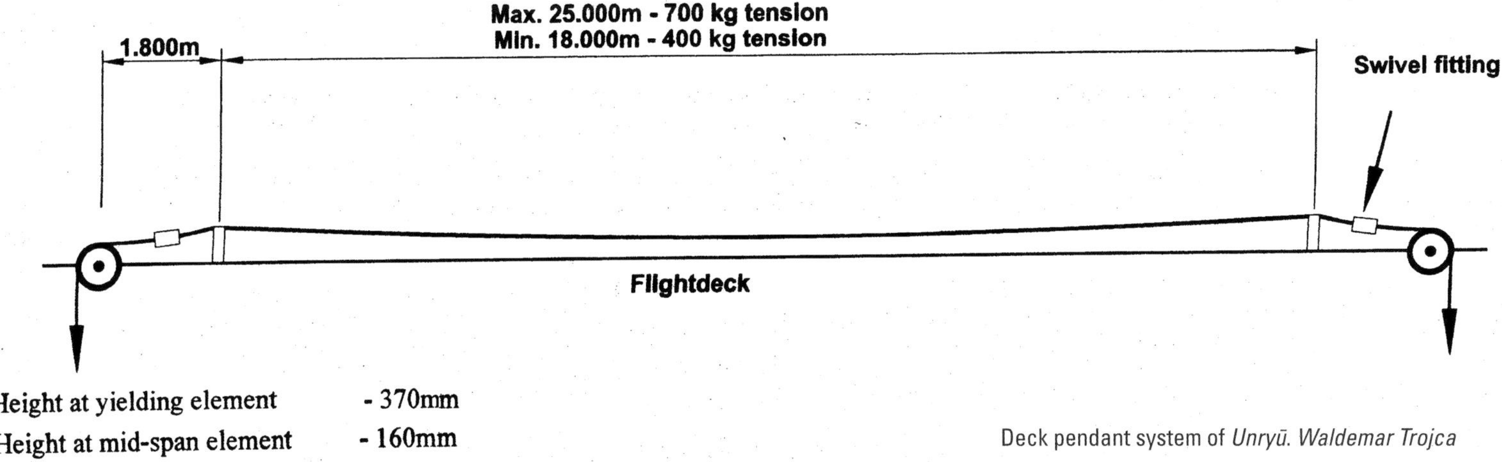

Deck pendant system of *Unryū*. *Waldemar Trojca*

Landing cycle. *Waldemar Trojca*

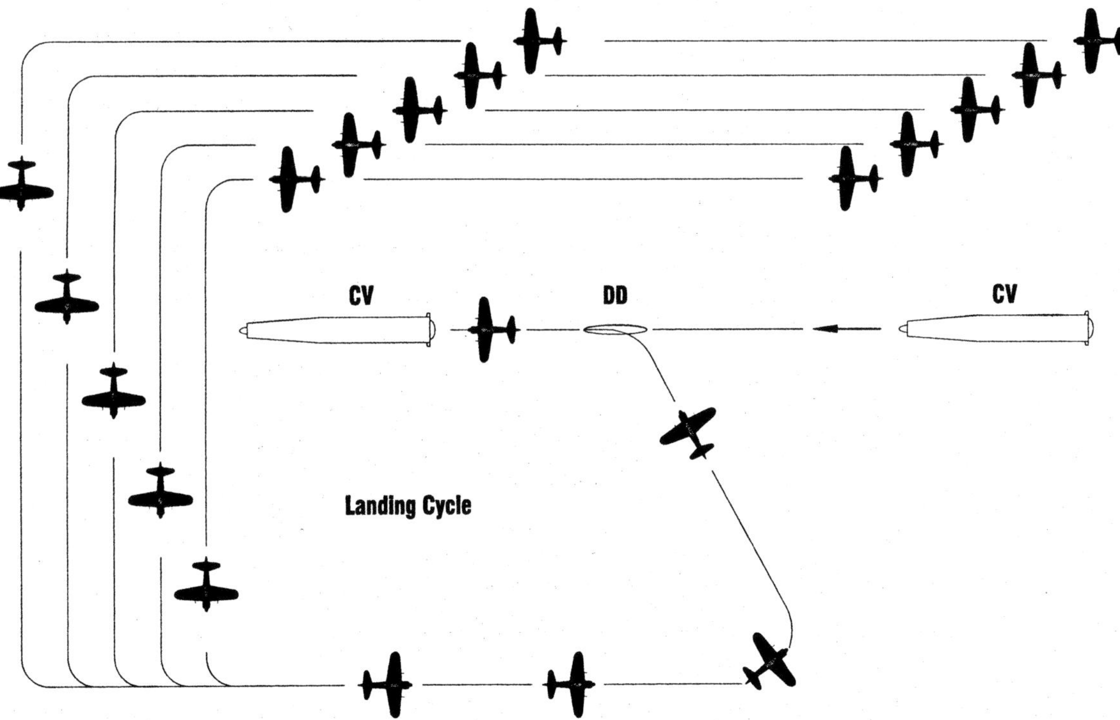

A type 97 carrier attack aircraft ("Kate") with landing hook down over *Sōryū* in the South China Sea in November–December 1939

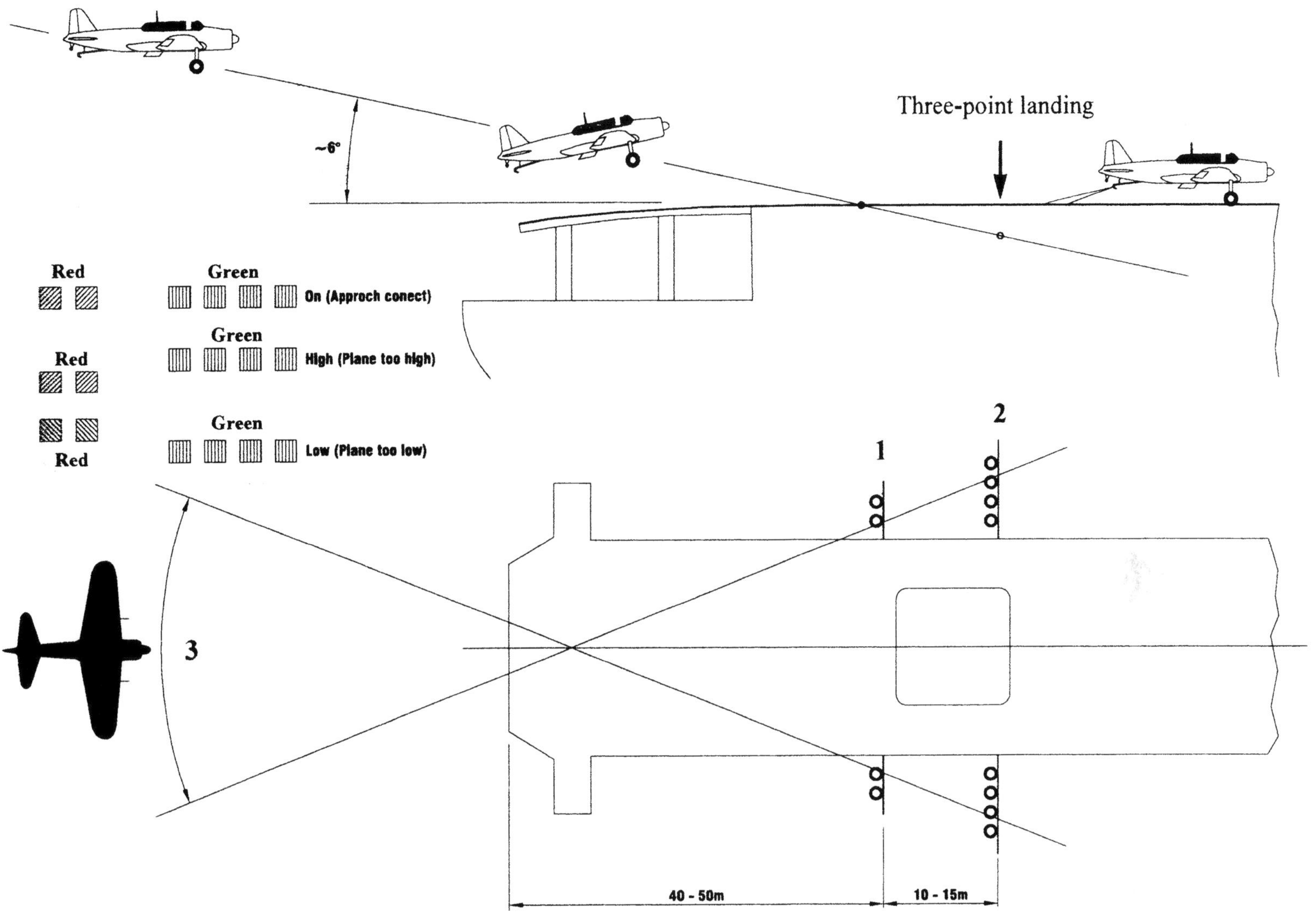

Landing approach, touchdown, and landing-light system. *Waldemar Trojca*

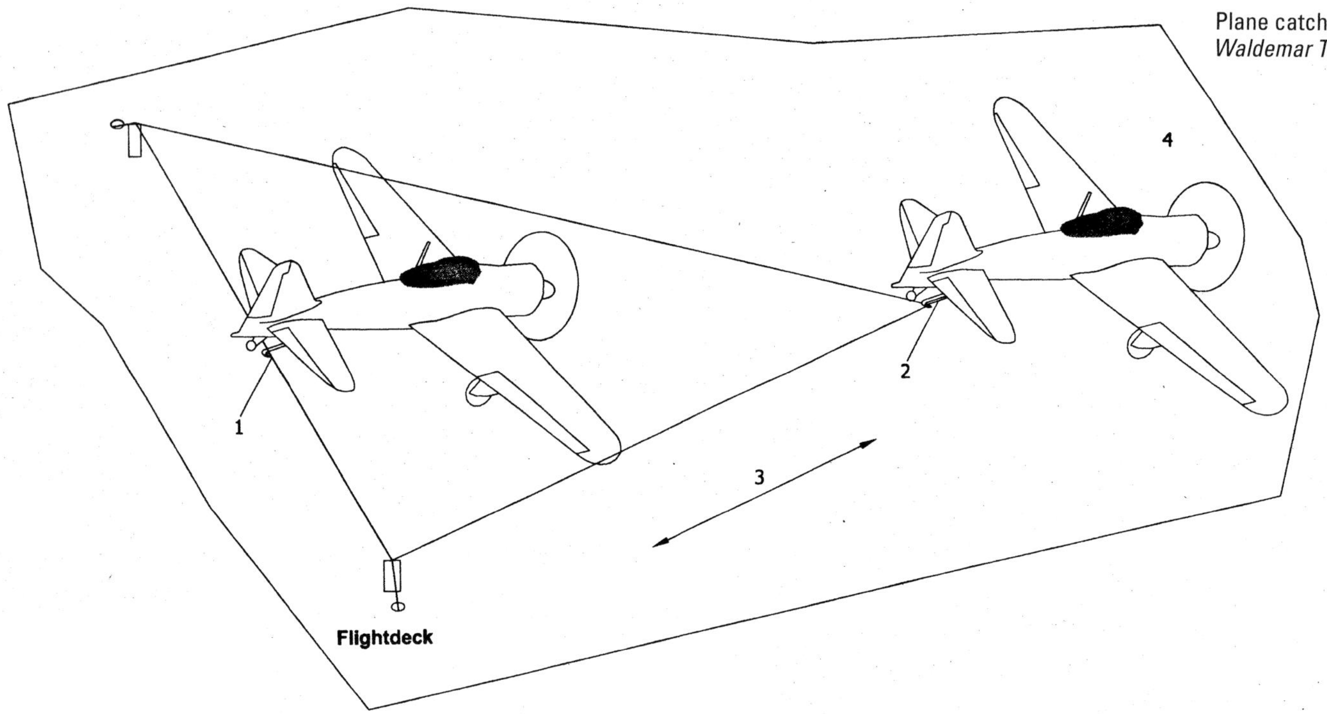

Plane catching a wire. *Waldemar Trojca*

4

2

1

3

Flightdeck

Crash Barrier

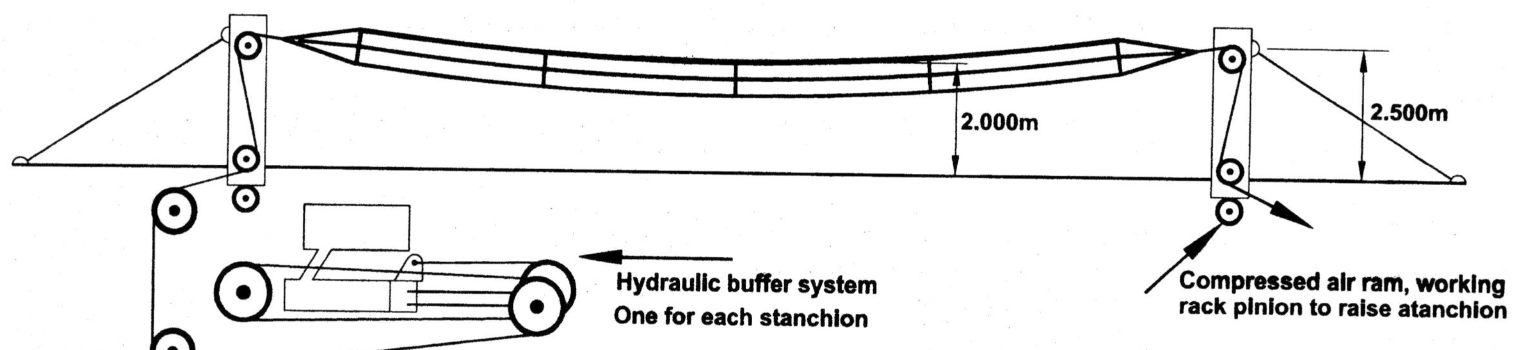

Crash barrier. *Waldemar Trojca*

CHAPTER 9

Weight Distributions

Sōryū* and *Hiryū					
Name	***Sōryū***			***Hiryū***	
Item	Tonnes	%	Tons	%	Tonnes
Hull	7,939/8,032.7	42.2/43.6	8,240/8,973.0	41.5/44.7	8,690
Fittings	1,527/1,154.7	/6.3	1,565/1,248.8	7.9/6.4	1.565
Armor	810/1,340.9	4.3/7.3	1,573/1,540.0	7.9/7.7	1,600
Protection	590/incl.	3.1/incl.	222/179.7	1.1/0.9	165
Permanent equipment	250/262.8	1.33/1.4	250/266.8	1.3/1.3	250
Consumable equipment	469/487.3	2.73/2.6	513/476.8	2.6/2.4	506
Guns	469.3/449.2	2.54/2.4	502/454.6	2.5/2.3	495.9
Torpedo	136.4/128.8	0.68/0.7	128/86.0	0.6/0.4	128.4
Electric	499.5/463.4	2.72/2.5	515/559.4	2.6/2.8	525
Aviation	660.8/662.6	3.52/3.6	676/559.4	3.4/2.8	668.8
Navigation	/9.4	/—	/9.0	/—	
Machinery	2,574.2/2,613.8	13.6/14.3	2,601/2,600.4	13.1/12.9	2,589.4
Fuel	2,270/2,162.7	12.1/11.7	2,500/2,504.1	12.6/12.5	2,500
Light oil (gasoline)	240/255.8	1.28/1.4	240/260.4	1.2/1.3	
Lubricating oil	34 + 24/68.2	/0.4	34 + 24/69.1	/0.3	
Reserve fresh water	100/124.8	0.53/0.7	100/119.3	0.5/0.6	
?	/339.5	/1.8			
Ballast	201.8/		177/68.3	/0.1	
Obscure weight	/–126.9	/–0.7	/–0.7	/—	
Total	18,800/18,447.7		19,860/20,096.9		20,250
$\frac{H}{L(B+D)}$	85.5		87.2		

Notes:
1. Weight of nautical instruments included in "Electric"
2. In case of "lubricating oil," the second weight is for planes.
3. Blank cells means no data available.

Source:
Fukuda, *Gunkan Kihon Keikaku Shiryō*, p. 42 (p. 68 for *Hiryū* column tonnes, taken from position of center of gravity data). Behind "/," "Weight of Center of Gravity Data for Miscellaneous Warships" by Preliminary Design Group, Lt. Tōyama, Engineer Imai, Assistant Engineers Takahashi & Ogino, second corrected and expanded edition, October 1941, p. 20.

	Katsuragi			
	Condition			
	Suppl. light load	**Trial**	**Full load**	**Light load**
(1) HULL AND ARMOR				
Hull	8,627.822	8,631.472	8,631.472	8,631.472
Armor	1,000.873	1,000.873	1,000.873	1,000.873
Protection	1,728.154	1,728.154	1,728.154	1,728.154
Fittings	953.908	954.878	954.878	954.878
Total	12,310.757	12,315.327	12,315.327	12,315.327
(2) FIXED EQUIPMENT				
Anchors, cables, hawsers	132.527	132.527	132.527	132.527
Masts, spars, rigging, etc.	63.524	64.027	64.027	64.027
Boats	47.934	47.934	47.934	47.934
Total	243.985	244.488	244.488	244.488
(3) BALLAST	341.857	341.857	341.857	341.857
(4) ORDNANCE (GUNNERY)				
High-angle guns (HAG)	179.542	180.852	180.852	180.852
Machine guns (MG)	86.305	130.961	130.961	130.961
Others for HAG + MG	0.113	11.911	11.911	11.911
Ammunition	—	221.496	221.496	—
Exercise ammunition	—	—	15.265	—
Fire control system	18.497	19.890	19.890	19.890
Others	0.087	7.035	7.035	0.423
Total	284.544	572.145	587.410	344.037
(5) TORPEDO AND TORPEDO EQUIPMENT				
Torpedo	73.572	127.147	141.001	95.694
Mine	3.733	10.686	10.732	1.180
Total	77.305	137.833	151.733	96.874
(6) NAVIGATION EQUIPMENT	13.348	13.871	13.871	9.511
(7) OPTICAL EQUIPMENT	10.010	11.665	11.665	11.665

	Condition			
	Suppl. light load	Trial	Full load	Light load
(8) ELECTRICAL EQUIPMENT				
Primary power plant	98.250	100.561	100.561	100.561
Secondary power plant	22.677	22.682	22.682	22.682
Searchlights	26.152	26.152	26.152	26.152
Deck illumination floodlights	26.985	27.076	27.076	27.076
Signal lights	2.466	2.466	2.466	2.466
Electrical training engines	37.891	37.919	37.919	37.919
Communications	53.780	55.971	55.971	55.971
Main units	36.805	36.805	36.805	36.805
Special-purpose units	14.192	15.122	15.122	15.122
Mixed-purpose units	38.137	38.234	38.234	38.234
Total	357.335	362.988	362.988	362.988
Radio	42.202	42.919	42.914	42.914
Hydrophone	2.642	9.392	9.392	9.392
Grand total	402.179	415.294	415.294	415.294
(9) AERONAUTICS				
Aircraft	0.043	173.155	174.530	26.910
	—	63.962	64.568	32.560
	—	200.214	200.214	2.200
Landing equipment	70.300	76.287	76.321	76.271
	5.537	74.139	74.468	73.483
Various equipment	56.582	62.178	62.178	62.178
Total	132.462	649.935	652.279	273.602

	Condition			
	Suppl. light load	**Trial**	**Full load**	**Light load**
(10) MACHINERY				
Main engines	466.281	474.053	474.053	474.053
Shafts and propellers	334.857	335.733	335.733	335.733
Boilers	535.913	541.612	541.612	541.612
Auxiliary engines	245.915	255.032	255.032	255.032
Uptakes and funnels	102.811	102.811	102.811	102.811
Valves, cocks, and pipes	435.526	447.534	447.534	447.534
Miscellaneous	173.078	191.881	191.881	191.881
Water in main condenser				
and overflow tank	69.200	45.515	68.273	—
Boiler feed water	89.824	89.824	89.824	—
	100.168	100.168	100.456	—
Lubricating oil in tank	16.800	9.780	9.780	—
Lubricating oil in engines + pipes	5.786	12.247	12.247	—
Total	2,576.159	2,606.201	2,629.247	2,348.661
(11) GENERAL EQUIPMENT				
Fixed equipment	37.860	50.000	50.000	50.000
Consumable equipment	6.354	24.600	36.900	—
Complement + property	88.200	186.600	186.600	186.600
Provisions	35.831	167.300	251.000	—
Canteen stores	8.800	3.300	5.000	—
Fresh water	78.600	153.952	230.928	—
Clothes	1.500	30.000	30.000	30.000
Medical stores	2.840	2.700	2.700	2.700
Documents (e.g., books)	0.550	0.500	0.500	0.500
Sanitary water	0.740	0.739	1.108	—
Total	261.275	619.691	794.736	269.800

	Condition			
	Suppl. light load	**Trial**	**Full load**	**Light load**
(12) FUEL				
Heavy oil in tanks	1,278.200	2,447.598	3,671.396	—
Light oil for boats	—	13.868	20.818	—
Light oil for aircraft	—	184.132	276.182	—
Light oil for torpedo				
preheater	—	1.377	2.050	—
Lubricating oil (excl. oil in				
engine + oil drain tank)	43.276	25.617	38.408	—
Lubricating oil for aircraft	—	21.939	32.802	—
Reserve feed water	152.000	117.691	176.536	—
Total	1,482.476	2,812.222	4,218.192	—
(13) OTHER				
Seawater in bilge keel	36.160	36.160	36.160	36.160
Emergency materials	8.000	8.000	8.000	8.000
Fresh water for hydrophone	63.370	63.370	63.370	—
Liquid for hangar fire				
extinguisher system	—	21.021	21.021	—
Margin	29.790	29.790	29.790	29.790
(14) GRAND TOTAL	18,505.000	20,898.870	22,534,440	16,746.072

CHAPTER 10

Propulsion Systems

General

Sōryū, *Hiryū*, *Unryū*, *Amagi*, *Kasagi*, and *Ikoma* had identical main engines and boilers, and the arrangement of the machinery spaces was also identical. For eight boilers there were eight boiler rooms, divided by a longitudinal bulkhead on the centerline and transverse bulkheads. The four main engines were also placed in four separate engine rooms, divided by longitudinal and transverse bulkheads. This arrangement was called "eight main boilers in eight boiler rooms and four main engines in four engine rooms" and became the standard type of large-sized high-speed ships at the end of the "treaty period" and continued as long as these ships were built during the Pacific War. Undoubtedly, this arrangement had some advantages. Since steam for one turbine set was always provided by two boilers, the distribution of power of each turbine could easily be unified, while simultaneously, the piping system and control of the whole machinery plant could be simplified. Because the eight boilers were divided well for split operation, this system was considered rational and ideal.

The main engines and main boilers of the six carriers above were exactly of the same types as those mounted in the heavy cruisers *Suzuya* and *Kumano*. With regard to the connection to the propeller shafts, the main difference was that in the heavy cruisers, the outboard engines were in the aft engine rooms and the inboard engines were in the forward engine rooms, while for the carriers, this unusual feature was given up and changed to the usual one, with the outboard engines situated in the forward engine rooms and the inboard engines in the aft ones.

Because of a shortage of material and workmen from 1944 onward, and the general insufficient capacity of the engine industry, the main engines and the main boilers could not be produced as speedily as needed. Therefore, *Katsuragi* and *Aso* were to be equipped with main engines and main boilers of the same type as those mounted in the antiaircraft destroyers of the Akizuki class. These ships had only 104,000 shp, as compared with the 152,000 shp of the other aircraft carriers, and their speed was reduced by about 2 knots to 32 knots.

Machinery of *Sōryū, Hiryū, Unryū, Amagi, Kasagi,* and *Ikoma*

The eight main boilers were large *Ro Gō Kampon Shiki* (Navy Technical Department type B), oil-burning, water-tube boilers fitted with air preheaters and superheaters, which were of "A" type, with the superheater in the middle of each bank and the air preheater over each bank. The fireroom was not under air pressure, since double casings with air pressure between were used. Steam pressure at superheater outlet was 22 bars, and steam temperature was 300°C. Each boiler produced 107 tons/h steam, and this output was the largest of all boiler types of the IJN.

The four main engines were Kampon-type steam turbines. Each set consisted of single high-pressure, intermediate-pressure, and low-pressure turbines, together with a speed-reduction gear system. The astern turbines were enclosed within the low-pressure turbine casings. Two cruising turbines were installed in the forward engine rooms and could be coupled individually to the high-pressure turbine pinion gear shaft by means of their cruising reduction gears and jaw clutches. The cruising turbine exhausted into the high-pressure turbine on the corresponding inboard shaft. For the inboard engines there were no cruising turbines.

The main engines developed 152,000 shp (153,000 in *Hiryū*). This output was surpassed only by the main engines of the carriers of the Shōkaku class and *Taihō*.

The main steam lines from the two forward boiler rooms on each side joined in the no. 3 and no. 4 boiler rooms, respectively, and led aft on the outboard side to the forward main turbines. The two aft boiler rooms (nos. 6 and 8, and nos. 5 and 7) on each side led aft on the inboard side, with each boiler through a separate line until it passed through the bulkhead of the engine rooms. Just aft of the bulkhead stops,[1] boilers nos. 6 and 8 joined, to feed the port inboard main turbines, and nos. 5 and 7 to supply the starboard inboard main turbines. A cross-connecting line led athwartship just aft of the boiler room bulkhead, connecting the main steam lines of all four shafts.

Main steam lines were made as straight as possible.

In each engine room, a cross-connection to the auxiliary steam line was provided. The auxiliary steam line operated at the same temperature and pressure as the main. This permitted cross-connection of the two systems in each space so as to receive all steam for the auxiliaries fitted in the engine room from the main steam in each space, if so desired.[2]

A cross-connection from port to starboard was provided only in the forward boiler rooms. When operating under split-plant condition, the bulkhead valve was closed.

There were four auxiliary exhaust systems. Two serviced the two forward boiler rooms on each side (nos. 2 and 4, and nos. 1 and 3). The other two systems served the two aft boiler rooms, one on each side. Between the forward and aft systems on each side, there was a cross-connection in each forward engine room. Another cross-connection was between the systems in the two aft engine rooms, and another for the forward engine rooms. There was also a connection between the lubrication oil pumps in the two forward engine rooms and those fitted in the aft engine rooms.

Trial Results of *Sōryū*, *Hiryū*, and *Unryū*

Condition	Displacement	Speed	hp	rpm	Effective hp	Propulsion efficiency
Sōryū						
10/10.5 overload power	18,621	35.217	160,326	339		
10/10 full power	18,871	34.898	152,483	333		
8/10	18,702	33.860	122,918	312		
6/10	18,756	32.189	92,094	287		
4/10	18,746	29.156	61,132	252		
3/10	18,715	26.511	41,022	229		
Standard	19,039	18.006	15,533	182		
Full astern	18,541		40,028	225		
Hiryū						
10/10 full power	20,346	34.28	152,733	326		
Standard	20,156	18.142	13,629	?		
10/10 final run	20,165	34.59	153,000	326	75.4	49.28%
Unryū						
10/10 full power	20,346	34.28	152,733	326	72.7	47.6
10/10 final run	20,165	34.59	153,000	326	75.4	49.28

Source:
Fukuda, *Gunkan Kihon Keikaku Shiryō*, pp. 113–114.

Machinery of *Katsuragi* and *Aso*

Because of the shortage of turbines originally planned for the Unryū class, *Katsuragi* and *Aso* mounted destroyer turbines and reduction gears as main propulsion machinery. Both were types used in the antiaircraft destroyers of the Akizuki class. The details of design followed a conventional pattern. Practically no attempt was made to use fabricated and welded steel plates. Single reduction gears persisted, and as a consequence the turbine speeds were much below those possible when double reduction gears were used. Size and weight increased accordingly. The main reasons were (1) lack of material, (2) lack of technical ability, and (3) development of the war situation.

The designed shaft horsepower per propulsion system was 104,000 divided among four shafts, or a total of minus 48,000 shp. The designed propeller revolutions per minute were 340.

The power transmitted to each shaft at the designed full speed, reduced to 32 knots, was divided among the high-pressure turbine (HPT), the intermediate-pressure turbine (IPT), and the low-pressure turbine (LPT), which formed one set of the main propulsion unit, each driving an independent pinion on main gearwheel. The HPT was at the aft end of the main reduction gear, while the IPT and LPT units were placed forward.

All three turbines of one set were of the impulse type. The HPT had a two-row Curtis wheel followed by two Rateau stages. The IPT had five Rateau stages, and the IPT was a double-flow engine with two two-row wheels on each side of the vertical centerline. The single astern turbine was located at the forward end of the LPT and consisted of a three-row, single-stage wheel.

A cross-compound cruising turbine (CRT) with a two-pinion single reduction gear was connected to the forward end of the IPT rotor. The connection was made through a disengaging-jaw-type clutch fitted with a mechanical synchronizing device.

Each propeller shaft was driven by a three-pinion reduction gear transmitting a total of 26,000 shp; the HPT and IPT were situated outboard, the LPT inboard. At the forward end of the LPT was a clutched, geared CRT having two pinions driven by a cross-compound turbine.

Both the cruising and main gears were of the single reduction type and followed the conventional pattern.

Auxiliary Turbines and Gears

The IJN developed three standard turbo-gear drives for such equipment as main feed pumps, fuel oil pumps, circulating pumps, blowers, etc. They were classified according to the main diameter of the blades on the single turbine wheel as 120, 180, and 270 mm machines.

Designed Horsepower and Maximum Revolutions per Minute		
Diameter (mm)	**Horsepower**	**rpm**
120	30	19,000
180	20–50	18,000
270	100–400	12,000

The designed steam conditions were 26.5 kg/cm^2 and 343°C with atmospheric back pressure.

Funnels and Hot-Smoke Cooling System

One of the outstanding features of Japanese aircraft carrier design was the uptake and funnel arrangement. All medium-sized aircraft carriers had curved funnels protruding out from the hull side slightly below the flight deck and then curved downward, so that the mouth was directed obliquely to the water surface. This arrangement was used in order to keep boiler flue gases from interfering with flight operations. When plane operations were conducted, the hot smoke had considerable effect on flight deck operating personnel and landing aircraft. Because the down-sweeping arrangement by itself was apparently not sufficient to obtain this, all classes dealt with in this book were equipped with a hot-smoke cooling system.

Power Installations

Even though the IJN decided to incorporate a 450 V, three-phase, fifty-cycle power plant in the design of future carriers, the completed ships of the #302 class had 225 V DC installations, because this equipment was available. In the modified #302 class, 450 V power plants were to be installed.

The capacity of the power plant was selected on the basis of calculated battle load. In the #302 class, the power plant was divided into five plants (two diesel and three turbine generators), while in the modified #302 class it was three diesel and two turbine generators.

The power plants were installed in the generator compartments fore and aft of the machinery spaces within the protected area. For the #302 class, a ring main distribution system was used, while an in-line switchboard radial-distribution system was to be installed in the modified #302 class.

Besides this system and numerous motor generators and transformers used for special applications such as radios, radars, heating, and galley equipment, the following principal secondary systems were installed in the Unryūs: (1) 220 V DC reserve power system, (2) 50 V, fifty-cycle AC system for selsyns, (3) 20 V DC system for telephones, and (4) 88 V DC system for searchlights and welding.

The reserve power system (emergency) was entirely battery powered and was used for a limited amount of equipment, primarily (1) steering, (2) one part of the radio equipment, (3) the gyrocompass, (4) signal and navigation lights, one part of the fire control system, and (5) fire pumps, which were also used for the foam firefighting system.

The #302 class ships had a 220 V DC reserve power system, while in the modified #302 class, a 100 V reserve power system was to be installed.

The secondary system for selsyns was supplied from generators driven by the 230 V turbogenerators of the primary power plant and was stepped down to 50 V.

The 88 V DC system for searchlights and welding consisted of one motor generator for arc supply for each of the four 110 cm searchlights.

The following table lists the primary and principal secondary power systems of the Unryū class. As for *Sōryū* and *Hiryū*, the authors failed to discover reliable data. It is supposed that these ships, with some exceptions, had a similar power installation. For instance, only DC was used, no foam firefighting system was installed, and welding was remarkably reduced.

Primary and Principal Secondary Power Systems of the *Unryū* Class

Item/Class	#302 Class	Modified #302 Class
Primary power plant	DC 225 V, 1,600 kW	AC 450 V, 2,350 kVA (75% power)
Diesel generator	200 kW × 2	550 kVA × 3
Turbogenerator	400 kW × 3	350 kVA × 2
Secondary power plant		
Batteries (reserve power)	320 Ah: 112 cells × 2 banks	320 Ah: 112 cells × 2 banks
	160 Ah: 112 cells × 1 bank*	160 Ah: 53 cells × 4 banks
Power for selsyn motors	Directly connected to turbogenerator	
	AC 230 V, 15 kVA × 3	AC 450 V, 15 kVA × 4
	M-G 230 V, 50 kVA × 1	M-G 450 V, 75 kVA × 1
Power for telephones	M-G DC 22 V, 3 kW × 2	same
	320 Ah: 11 cells × 2 banks	same
Power for searchlights	17.6 kW at 88 V DC × 4	same
Distribution system	Ring main	In-line SWBD** radial
Lighting voltage	220	100

Notes:
* 160 Ah used for steering only; ** SWBD = switchboard

Sōryū during trials off Tateyama on January 22, 1938. After being handed over to Yokosuka, she ran trials on the measured mile between Iwafukuro and Ukishima.

Another view of *Sōryū* during trials off Tateyama on January 22, 1938. The ship is undergoing 8/10 power tests prior to the 10/10 (full) power tests on the measured mile.

Hiryū during her final trials off Tateyama on June 21, 1939. Type 94 directors are in place, and two 110 cm searchlights are raised.

Hiryū during 10/10 power trials off Tateyama on June 21, 1939

A view of *Sōryū* in 1937, showing a 9 m cutter, no. 5 (third on the starboard side) high-angle gun, and smoke-protected 25 mm mounts. The tips of the funnels are not yet painted black.

Almost the same view as the previous one, but during full-power trials in December 1937. The funnel tips are now black, and white smoke shows that the hot-smoke cooling system is operating. Arresting wires are visible.

Kasagi's starboard side with the two funnels. *Naval Historical Center*

Aboard *Kasagi* on October 19, 1945. In the background is the minelayer *Kamishima*. *Naval Historical Center*

CHAPTER 11

Illumination, Signaling, and Navigation

The lighting circuits involved essentially four circuits: (1) normal lighting, (2) working lighting, (3) alarm lighting, and (4) emergency lighting.

Normal lighting was the general lighting throughout all compartments that required lighting. As a result of several shortcomings, officers and ratings lived and worked, except for these spaces with outside illumination, in a region of perpetual gloom.

The work lighting was a circuit that supplemented the normal lighting in the essential machinery spaces, the hangars, and some repair rooms. In the hangars there were also provided hand lights and small searchlights to improve both circuits when necessary.

The alarm lighting was a circuit that included all lighting outside compartments, and also all the interior lights that could not be blacked out immediately.

The emergency lighting circuit was usually operated by the normal service power, but upon loss of this, it was manually transferred to battery power. It was a circuit that was to provide lighting in the vital parts only.

The navigation lights conformed to the International Rules of the Road, but no range light was used.

The usual blinkers and the mast top 360° lights were provided for transmitting code. In the Unryūs, infrared signaling equipment for IFF (identification friend or foe) was also used.

Four arrays of colored lights were used for recognition and signaling, located at the stern and the signal mast. The arrays consisted of red, green, and white lights, whose relative position could be changed at will.

The ships outlined in this book were also equipped with battle lanterns of the 6 V, lead storage battery type. Sixty lanterns were distributed in the ship during battle cruising and were returned to a central location for recharging.

Because the IJN had no radar-directed fire control system, the crews depended on searchlights to find attacking planes and warships at night. Illumination of the flight deck at night was another duty. They were equipped with a considerable number of searchlights used not only for illumination but also signaling.

Searchlights

Item/Ship	*Sōryū* and *Hiryū*	*Unryū* Class
Type 96 110 cm searchlight, model 1, for 220 V	—	4 (according to *Katsuragi's* official data book, only 3)
Type 92 110 cm searchlight, model 3	4	—
Type 94 searchlight director, model 1	4	—
Type 96 searchlight director, model 2	—	4 (as above, only 3)
60 cm signal searchlight, model 1, for 220 V	2	2
20 cm signal searchlight, model 1, for AC 50 V	2	2 (as above, 4)
2 kW signal lamp, model 1, model 2, for 220 V	2	2
Infrared signaling equipment	—	1 set

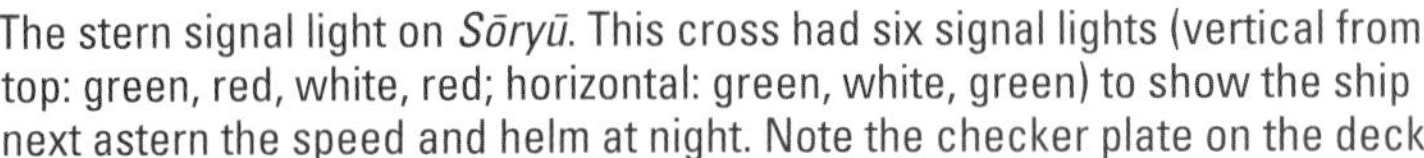

The stern signal light on *Sōryū*. This cross had six signal lights (vertical from top: green, red, white, red; horizontal: green, white, green) to show the ship next astern the speed and helm at night. Note the checker plate on the deck.

Sōryū's signal mast has been tilted during trials. Note the wind sleeve and the minesweeper that is acting as plane guard, ready to pick up downed pilots.

CHAPTER 12

Interior Communication Systems

A total of twenty-seven interior communication systems (IC) (alarms, telephones, telegraphs, announcing, public address, recording, electric clocks and indicators, call bells, voice tubes, etc.) were installed to provide communication and operate an aircraft carrier in peace and war. Some were quite extensive and complex, while others were apparently inadequate. To the first category belonged the telegraph system as well as the sound power telephone damage-control circuit, and the emergency telephone circuit, while in the second category the battery-powered telephone system may be cited as an example. Lack of space prevents dealing with these systems, the majority of which referred to navigation, but a few remarks will follow with regard to aircraft and two systems outlined (the hot-smoke cooling system also belonged to the IC systems but is described elsewhere).

An IC system generally consisted of one or two master station units and ten to sixteen speaker microphone stations and was installed, for example, between the bridge and the ready room (for air crews) and between the bridge and the antiaircraft defense post (open bridge).

The call bell system was used in conjunction with telephones and voice tubes and was installed in several groups, one of which was aircraft control. In the Unryū class, about 600 telephones, both battery and sound powered, were installed, and of those, some belonged to the direct and special exchange systems, of which one circuit provided direct communication instructions for aircraft.

A gyro repeater and two 12 cm binoculars fitted with gyro repeaters were installed in the flight control station.

CHAPTER 13

Complement

Complement			
Item/Ships	***Sōryū* Class**	***Unryū* Class**	***Katsuragi***
Source	Directive 169 of 23 April 1937, amendment 784, 1941	Directive 1994 of 25 September 1943, amendment 2154, 1944	Official Ship's Data Book of 4 November 1944
Officers	53	61	48 (+ 24 as flagship)
Special-service officers	29	37	40
Cadets	—	—	56
Warrant officers	43	56	1,432
Petty officers	292	375	
Seamen	686	1,042	
Total	1,103	1,571	1,576 (1,600 as flagship)

Capt. Yokokawa Ichihei and his officers of *Hiryū* photographed by the island structure while off Tateyama in the summer of 1940. *Courtesy of Nakagawa Tsutomu*

CHAPTER 14
Operational Histories

Sōryū

Participated in the China Incident from April 1938 until April 1939 and took part in the Amoy, Daya Bay, and Nanning operations. On December 15, 1938, incorporated into 2nd Fleet (*Dai 2 Kantai*), 2nd Carrier Division (*Dai 2 Kōkū Sentai*) (RAdm. Totsuka Michitarō; from November 1, 1940, RAdm. Yamaguchi Tamon). On April 10, 1941, incorporated into 1st Air Fleet (*Dai 1 Kōkū Kantai*), 2nd Carrier Division. Took part in the invasion of southern French Indochina in the summer of 1941. Flagship 2nd Carrier Division, August 11, 1941. On December 7, 1941, the Pearl Harbor attack and later the attack on Wake Island. On February 19, 1942, the Port Darwin attack. Supported the operations off Java. Operated in the Bay of Bengal in March–April 1942 and participated in the sinking of HMS *Dorsetshire*, HMS *Cornwall*, and HMS *Hermes*. Sunk on June 4, 1942, at the Battle of Midway, after being hit by three bombs from US carrier planes. At 1913, *Sōryū* went down, taking with it 711 crew, including her CO. Removed from register on August 10, 1942.

Commanding officers	
August 16, 1937	Beppu Akitomo
December 1, 1937	Teraoka Kinpei
November 15, 1938	Uwano Keizō
October 15, 1939	Yamada Sadayoshi
October 15, 1940	Kamase Wataru
November 25, 1940	Kosaka Kanae
September 12, 1941	Hasegawa Kiichi
October 6, 1941	Yanagimoto Ryūsaku

Hiryū

On November 15, 1939, incorporated into 2nd Fleet, 2nd Carrier Division (with *Sōryū*), flagship. Participated in the China Incident in 1940–1941, including the Hainan operations. Took part in the invasion of southern French Indochina in the summer of 1941. On August 11, 1941, incorporated into 1st Air Fleet, 2nd Carrier Division. On December 7, 1941, the Pearl Harbor attack and later the attack on Wake Island. On February 19, 1942, the Port Darwin attack. Supported the operations off Java. Operated in the Bay of Bengal in March–April 1942 and participated in the sinking of HMS *Dorsetshire*, HMS *Cornwall*, and HMS *Hermes*. Flagship 2nd Carrier Division (RAdm. Yamaguchi Tamon) from April 10, 1942. Sunk on June 5, 1942, at the Battle of Midway, after being seriously damaged by four bombs from US carrier planes the day before. Probably soon after 0900, *Hiryū* went down, taking with it 389 crew members, including her CO. Removed from register on September 25, 1942.

Commanding officers	
April 1, 1939	Takenaka Ryūzō
November 15, 1939	Yokokawa Ichihei
November 15, 1940	Yano Shikazō
September 8, 1941	Kaku Tomeo

Unryū

On August 6, 1944, incorporated into 3rd Fleet, 1st Carrier Division. On October 30, 1944, flagship of Mobile Fleet (*Kidō Butai*) (VAdm. Ozawa Jisaburō). On December 15, 1944, Mobile Fleet abolished and incorporated into Combined Fleet (*Rengō Kantai*), 1st Carrier Division. Then used for emergency transport operations. On December 19, 1944, during transport mission to Manila, via northern Senkaku Archipelago, hit by two torpedoes from submarine USS *Redfish* 230 nautical miles north-northwest of Miyako-jima. Sank about 1700, taking with it 1,235 crew members, including her CO. Removed from register on February 20, 1945.

Commanding officers	
August 6, 1944	Konishi Kaname

Amagi

On August 10, 1944, flagship of Mobile Fleet (VAdm. Ozawa Jisaburō). On December 15, 1944, incorporated into Combined Fleet, 1st Carrier Division (RAdm. Obayashi Sueo), flagship. On March 1, 1945, incorporated into 2nd Fleet (VAdm. Itō Seiichi), 1st Carrier Division. Never left the Inland Sea. On March 19, 1945, damaged by US carrier planes at Kure. On April 13, 1945, moored at Mitsugojima. On April 20, 1945, classified as special-duty reserve ship. From July 24 to 28, 1945, seriously damaged by US carrier planes. Flooding increased the next day, and ship listed and settled on the bottom. On November 20, 1945, removed from register. Refloated on July 31, 1947, and dismantled at Harima Zōsen Kure Senkyo, which was completed on December 11, 1947. Part of the hull became a floating railway lighter at Hakodate.

Commanding officers	
August 10, 1944	Yamamori Kamenosuke
October 23, 1944	Miyazaki Toshio
April 20, 1945	Hiratsuka Shirō

Katsuragi

On December 15, 1944, incorporated into Combined Fleet, 1st Carrier Division. On June 1, 1945, attached to Combined Fleet. Never left the Inland Sea. On March 19, 1945, damaged by US carrier planes at Kure. On March 24, 1945, moored at Mitsugojima. From July 24 to 28, 1945, seriously damaged by US carrier planes. Flight deck essentially wrecked, but ship remained afloat. On October 5, 1945, removed from register. On December 1, 1945, designated a special-transport warship and used as repatriation ship. From December 22, 1946, to November 30, 1947, dismantled at Hitachi Zōsen Sakurajima Zōsen.

Commanding officers	
October 15, 1944	Kawabata Masaharu
April 1, 1945	Hiratsuka Shirō
April 20, 1945	Miyazaki Toshio
October 3, 1945	Miyazaki Toshio
February 11, 1946	Ōhara Toshimichi
July 25, 1946	Tamura Kiyoshi
August 19, 1946	Ōhara Toshimichi

Kasagi

On April 1, 1945, work suspended when carrier was 84 percent complete. On April 25, 1945, towed to Sasebo. From September 21, 1946, to December 31, 1947, dismantled at Sasebo Senpaku Kōgyō.

Aso

On November 9, 1944, work suspended when carrier was 60 percent complete. In July 1945, used for rocket tests (*Sakura dan*). Flooded inside Kurahashijima and settled on the bottom. From December 31, 1946, to April 26, 1947, raised and dismantled at Harima Zōsen Kure Senkyo.

Ikoma

On November 9, 1944, work suspended when carrier was 60 percent complete. On November 17, 1944, launched and moved to Shōdoshima, Ikeda Bay. From June 4, 1946, to March 10, 1947, dismantled at Mitsui Zōsen Tamano Zōsen.

Sōryū (*right*) and *Ryūjō* anchored in Ise Bay in September 1938. They constituted the 2nd *Kōkū Sentai*, commanded by RAdm. Samejima Tomoshige.

Sōryū photographed from the Italian light cruiser *Bartolomeo Colleoni* off Tsingtao, China, on March 28, 1939. Together with *Ryūjō Sōryū* formed the 2nd *Kōkū Sentai. Courtesy of Eugen Pinak*

Sōryū and *Ryūjō* in Tokyo Bay around 1938. The port 12.7 cm high-angle guns look almost white in this view. The plane is a type 95 reconnaissance seaplane ("Dave").

Sōryū in Ariake Bay in April 1939, photographed from the destroyer *Oboro*

Sōryū photographed in 1939, from the destroyer *Murakumo. Sekai no Kansen*

Sōryū in Staring Bay, Celebes, on February 22, 1942, after the Port Darwin attack, photographed from the heavy cruiser *Haguro*. *Sōryū* has type 99 carrier bombers on the flight deck, and mantlets around her bridge structure. To the left is *Kaga*.

Sōryū, *Kaga* (*behind*), and the heavy cruiser *Nachi* in Staring Bay on February 22, 1942

A photo from the heavy cruiser *Atago* shows part of VAdm. Nagumo Chūichi's force in Staring Bay on February 22, 1942. *From left*: Heavy cruiser *Chikuma*, *Sōryū*, a tanker, *Hiryū*, and the heavy cruiser *Takao*. *Courtesy of Dan Kaplan*

The commanding officer of the 2nd *Kōkū Sentai*, RAdm. Yamaguchi Tamon (*in chair second from left*), is relaxing on the flight deck of *Sōryū* after returning to Staring Bay, in March 1942.

VAdm. Nagumo's *Kidō Butai* at the height of its power is here leaving Staring Bay on March 26, 1942. Astern of *Akagi* follows *Sōryū*, *Hiryū*, *Hiei*, *Kirishima*, *Haruna*, *Kongō*, *Zuikaku*, and *Shōkaku* (partly visible).

Sōryū (*left*) and *Hiryū* (*right*) as seen from the battleship *Kongō* in April 1942, after completing the Ceylon Operation

Said to be a photo of *Sōryū* and *Hiryū* en route to Midway

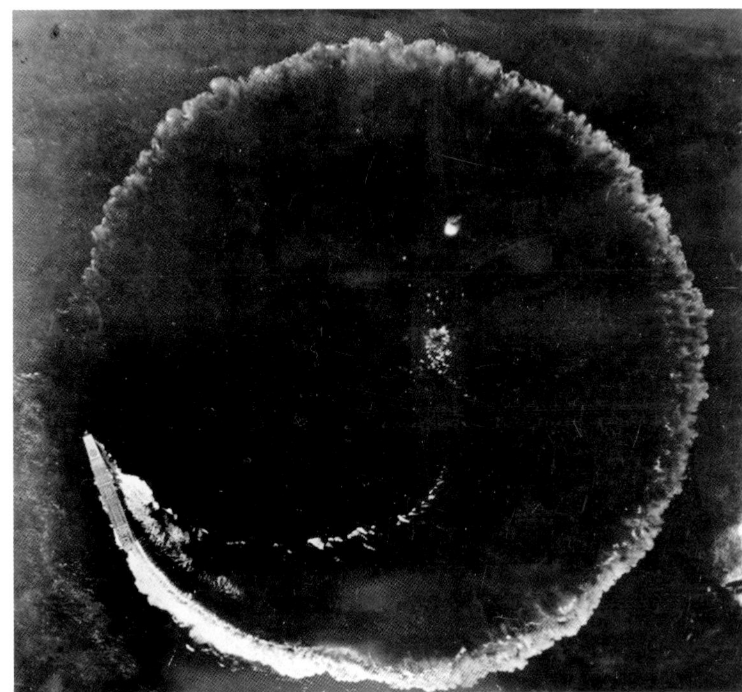

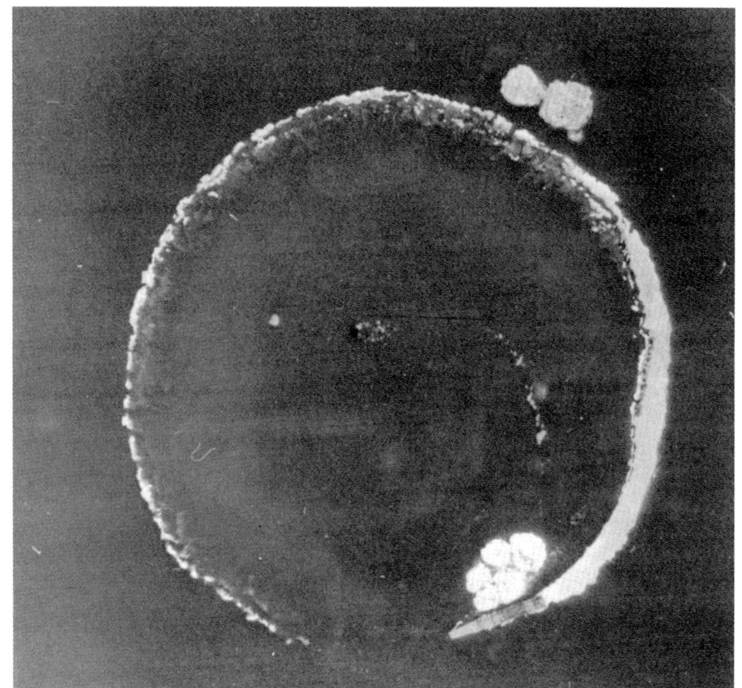

Sōryū is evading bombs from US B-17s during the Battle of Midway on June 4, 1942. Note that there are no aircraft on deck. *Naval Historical Center*

Hiryū at Yokosuka on July 5, 1939. At 1300, VAdm. Araki Hikosuke, of the Yokosuka Navy Yard, handed over the ship to Capt. Takenaka Ry*ūzō*. Note the ceremonial Shinto trees and curtain forward of the bridge, behind which ceremonies took place.

Hiryū in Kagoshima Bay in October 1941, during preparations for the Hawaiian Operation

Scene from the special naval review off Yokohama on October 11, 1940. *Hiryū* had participated in the occupation of French Indochina and returned to Japan via Sanya, Hainan Island. From the left are the battleships *Kongō*, *Mutsu*, and *Nagato*. *Hiryū* (*to the right*) and *Sōryū* are faintly visible in the background.

View from *Hiryū*'s flight deck off Yokohama on October 11, 1940. *Sōryū* is just forward of *Hiryū* and to left is the battleship *Yamashiro*.

A type 97 carrier attack aircraft ("Kate") takes off from *Hiryū* while en route to Midway, May 31–June 1, 1942. The photo was probably take from the oiler *Kyokutō Maru.*

Hiryū under attack from US B-17 bombers on June 4, 1942. Three "Zero" fighters are on deck, and note the large *hinomaru* painted forward and the *katakana* for "HI" aft. *Naval Historical Center*

Hiryū in flames on the morning of June 5, 1942. It was photographed from an altitude of 200 m by an aircraft from *Hōshō*.

Another view of the burning *Hiryū*. The forward part of the flight deck is shattered, and part of the forward elevator almost leans against the island.

Unryū prepared for trials off Yokosuka on July 16, 1944. Additional machine guns and 12 cm rocket launchers have been added. The anti-submarine color scheme used colors No. 2 and 21

The last of the *Unryū* as seen from the periscope of USS *Redfish* at 1657 on December 19, 1944. The port "wing" (landing mark) and sponsons can be seen.

Amagi (*left*) and the escort carrier *Kaiyō* (*right*) under attack from US carrier planes at Kure on March 19, 1945. *Amagi* was hit by one or two bombs to starboard aft. *Courtesy of Eugen Pinak*

Amagi is seriously damaged by US carrier planes at Kure on July 24, 1945. Note the camouflage netting.

Amagi photographed by US aircraft after the attack on July 28, 1945. Her flight deck is completely shattered. Note *Katsuragi* at the top. *Courtesy of Eugen Pinak*

Amagi was bombed by US aircraft in late July 1945, and on July 29 she capsized to port.

Amagi resting at the bottom off Mitsugojima, Kure, on 8 October 8, 1945. *Courtesy of Eugen Pinak*

Amagi off Mitsugojima on June 1, 1946. She was finally refloated on July 31, 1947, and scrapped.

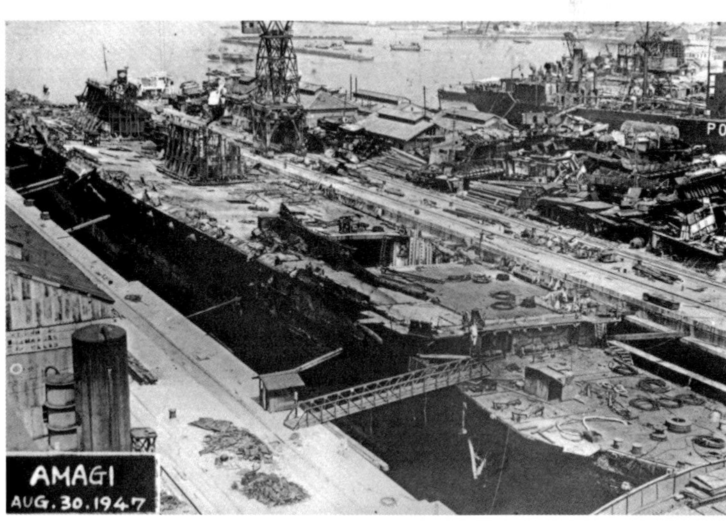

Amagi is being scrapped on August 30, 1947, at Kure. The flight deck is removed and the upper hangar is visible.

The camouflaged *Katsuragi* off Mitsugojima during the air attack on July 24, 1945.

Katsuragi moored off Mitsugojima on October 8, 1945. Note the damaged flight deck. *Courtesy of Eugen Pinak*

Overhead view of *Katsuragi* off Mitsugojima in 1945

Katsuragi's damaged flight deck is being inspected by the Allies.

A view from *Katuragi's* damaged hangar deck. *US National Archives*

Katsuragi on October 8, 1945. From this view she appears almost undamaged. *US National Archives*

Katsuragi in 1945 prior to her conversion into a repatriation ship. *Courtesy of Dan Kaplan*

Katsuragi undergoing emergency repairs at Kure in 1945, before being used as a repatriation ship. Note the Japanese flag painted on the hull plating.

Katsuragi in Osaka in January 1946.

Katsuragi at Kure at the end of 1945. On October 2, she had been designated a special-transport ship for use as a repatriation ship. Her name is painted on the hull side.

Katsuragi at Kurihama in April 1946. Her flight deck was closed as it was, and it could be very hot in the hangars. As can be seen, temporary ventilation was fitted.

Katsuragi in 1946. Note the temporary ventilation.

After repatriation journeys, *Katsuragi* has entered Hitachi Zōsen Sakurajima, Osaka, for demolition. Between January and November 1946, she visited Wewak, Torokina, Rabaul, Saigon, Saint-Jacques, Lembang, Medan, Singapore, and Bangkok, to mention a few.

Katsuragi at Osaka on November 20, 1946, awaiting demolition

Katsuragi on August 30, 1947, when being demolished at Hitachi Zōsen Sakurajima, Osaka. It began on December 22, 1946, was finished on November 30, 1947, and generated 11,000 tons of scrap metal.

Kasagi on November 2, 1945, in Ebisu Bay. The submarines beyond are *I 156*, *I 157*, *I 159*, and *Ro 50*. *Kure Maritime Museum*

Kasagi in Sasebo Shipyards no. 4 dock on August 31, 1946, ready to be dismantled. Note the numerous aircraft tie-down points on the flight deck. To the right is the former battleship *Shikishima*.

Kasagi's stern, with the large emergency rudder lashed to port

Kasagi being demolished between September 1, 1946, and December 31, 1947. *Courtesy of Eugen Pinak*

Aso at Kure on December 20, 1946. She had been used as a target for rockets on July 20, 1945, and is here about to be towed for breakup. *Courtesy of Eugen Pinak*

Aso was refloated and towed to Kure for scrapping. On December 21, 1946, the work began, and here plates above the funnel are being removed.

Aso's flight deck and the uppermost deck have been removed, and the lower hangar is exposed. Dismantling was finished on April 26, 1947.

Ikoma at Shodōshima, Eastern Inland Sea, on May 23, 1946. Due to a mistake, the shades above and below the waterline were different.

The unfinished *Ikoma* on January 14, 1946. Two funnels have been loaded, and rainwater has caused a starboard list.

Endnotes

Chapter 1

1. For this class, see Hans Lengerer, "The Aircraft Carriers of the *Shōkaku* Class," in *Warship 2015*, ed. John Jordan (London: Conway, 2015), 90–109, which has some excellent drawings by Michael Wünschmann.
2. Restricted to items referring to aircraft carriers.
3. However, France and Italy did not ratify this treaty.
4. For this ship, see Hans Lengerer, "The IJN Light Carrier *Ryūjō*," in *Warship 2014*, ed. John Jordan (London: Conway, 2014), 129–145.
5. We have not found an explanation of the reasons why the carrier was stricken, but in my opinion the building of a carrier of less than 10,000 tons had lost its raison d'être, because it had to be added to the total tonnage and would have left 2,780 tons, "useable for nothing."

Chapter 2

1. This method had already been recommended in Secret Document No. 215 of 1932. The principle of individual superiority brought about, for example, the super battleships of the Yamato class, the aircraft carriers of the Shōkaku class, and destroyers and submarines in the Third Naval Replenishment Program of 1937 and was continued with the same class of battleships, the aircraft carrier *Taihō*, and, again, destroyers and submarines in the Fourth Naval Completion Program of 1939.
2. When it became certain that *Ryūjō* had to be added to the total tonnage, the Naval General Staff required an increase of planes by 50%—to thirty-six from twenty-four.
3. When the *Sōryū* was commissioned, her standard displacement was 15,900 tons. Even though both aircraft and artillery had been remarkably reduced and speed and range had been decreased, 5,850 tons or roughly 57% of the originally planned 10,050 tons were necessary to obtain an operable carrier. This makes obvious how much the Naval General Staff had exaggerated the armament required for the designs: G 6, the initial requirement for *Sōryū*, and the corrected version, which was designed as G 8.
4. This argument has the defect that everybody who knows something about shipbuilding can see, and those who were aware of the requirements would immediately have realized that no ship of this displacement could have been built fulfilling these requirements.
5. No carrier was actually built to this design for *Akagi*'s small vertical funnel, which, prior to conversion, came out at the hull side and not on the flight deck.
6. This may be an expression of the recognition that the length of the flight deck (194 m in G 6) was too short. For instance, when converting the *Kaga*, a flight deck stretched over the whole length of the hull had been required.
7. When the requirement to mount 15.5 cm guns was roughly inspected, the standard displacement had been calculated as about 14,000 tons, rather more.
8. Such a delay was not uncommon with the ships of this program. It should have been completed on March 31, 1937, but the capacity of the Japanese shipyards, occupied with stability improvement measures after the *Tomozuru* Incident and then strengthening measures after the 4th Fleet Incident and also the modernization conversion of battleships, heavy cruisers, and the carriers *Kaga* and *Akagi*, was insufficient to manage the rapid increase of work. To mention some more delays: the aircraft carrier *Hiryū*, sixteen

months; the heavy cruiser *Chikuma*, fourteen months; the seaplane tenders of the Chitose class, nine months; and the fast tanker *Takasaki*, thirty-three months.

9. Adding political and psychological viewpoints, the first designs may have expressed the mood after the conclusion of the London Treaty, the Manchurian Incident, the Shanghai Incident, and the crises between Japan and the United States after invading part of China.
10. As a consequence, the beam of the hull had to be increased (by 0.7 m at the waterline). This, in turn, resulted in the change (adaptation) of the lines, increase of displacement, and also a slightly deeper draft. This is pointed out here only as an example in order to illustrate that the change of one principal dimension can bring about far-reaching consequences, which are often simply overlooked.
11. Besides the heightening of the bridge by one deck (to provide the same view over the bow—necessary due to the change of the bridge's position), the construction below the bridge affected the form of the outer hull and also influenced the shape of the upper hangar compared with the *Sōryū*.

Chapter 3

1. See also Hans Lengerer, "*Katsuragi* and the Failure of Mass Production of Medium Sized Aircraft Carriers," in *Warship 2010*, ed. John Jordan (London: Conway, 2010), 103–121; and *Illustrated Record of the Transition of the Superstructures of BB Kongō Class & Introduction to CV Unryū Class* (Katowice, Poland: Model Hobby, 2010).
2. Actually the vice chief of the Naval General Staff and the vice navy minister had conferred about this program already in July 1941 (Naval General Staff top secret #377, dated July 28, 1941), and the construction of the first ships started as early as September 1941, while the budget was permitted in the 79th and 81st sessions of the Diet (opened December 26, 1941, and December 26, 1942, respectively). In his proposal "On Shipbuilding in Wartime and Reinforcement of Air Strength in Fiscal Year 1941" (Naval General Staff top secret #533 of November 6, 1941) to the navy minister, the chief of the Naval General Staff had designated this program as "Additional Shipbuilding of 1941 for Wartime."
3. Of course, this would have required a remarkable change of the building policy and the immediate stop of large warships in order to attain building capacity. The IJN would also have been forced to expand capacities for the construction of aviation facilities, revise existing training programs, etc. It is very easy to state "mass production" of one type but very hard to execute it in view of Japan's restricted building capacity. On the other hand, it provided the recognition of the absolute necessity, which can, at least, be doubted before the Battle of Midway.
4. It was later included in the 1942 Modified Wartime Warship Replenishment Program (*Shōwa 17 Nendo Senji Kansen Hojū Keikaku*) or the Modified Fifth Program (*Kai Maru Gō Keikaku*), which was a total revision of the Fifth Naval Armament Replenishment Program.
5. Fifteen Unryūs (#5001 to #5015) were included in the initial planning, but as a result of the decision to convert the incomplete battleship *Shinano* into an aircraft carrier, two ships allocated to Yokosuka Navy Yard were canceled, reducing the total to thirteen ships, or fourteen ships when *Unryū* is included.

Chapter 5

1. Named after the Austrian naval engineer Fritz F. Maier.
2. However, *Katsuragi* had 3,750 mm due to less shp.
3. See, for instance, Hans Lengerer, "The Japanese Destroyers of the *Hatsuharu* Class," in *Warship 2007*, ed. John Jordan (London: Conway, 2007), 91–110, particularly 98–99.
4. It is supposed that *Sōryū*'s bilge keels were the same, but the authors are lacking data.
5. The *Tomozuru* Incident, the investigation of the stability of Japanese warships and the series of measures taken to improve stability, is outlined in Hans Lengerer, "The *Tomozuru* Incident," in *Warship 2011*, ed. John Jordan (London: Conway, 2011), 148–164.

Chapter 6

1. For more on IJN fire protection, see Lars Ahlberg & Hans Lengerer, *Taihō*, vol. 1 (Gdańsk, Poland: AJ-Press, 2004), 63–76.

Chapter 8

1. Zinc powder in a solution of sodium silicate.
2. The IJN never tried to develop an accelerator such as those used by, for example, the USN. Catapulting seaplanes from these ships required much time until the plane and its carriage were on the catapult. From this point of view, it is hardly understandable why the IJN wanted to use the same method on carriers, which would delay instead of accelerate takeoff operations.
3. The primary difficulty was the excessive cable slap.
4. *Katsuragi*'s official data book also gives four arresting engines but three type 3, model 10, and one type 3, model 11. The arrester wires are stated as being the Kure type, but production of this type stopped when the type 3 was completed. Therefore,

it is very unlikely that *Katsuragi* was fitted with the Kure type while the earlier completed sisters had type 3. When evaluating such data, one must never forget that from the end of 1944, the IJN's administration showed signs of dispersal, and differences between planning and reality became all too common.

5. The first three were more or less experimental models, and after executing improvements, model 4 was completed in 1935 and fitted on aircraft carriers.
6. Report A-11 of the US Naval Technical Mission to Japan states that securing points were provided by ring bolts in the painted (*Hiryū*) and the unpainted (Unryū class) steel decks.
7. Report A-11 also says that "The upper hangar was divided by athwartship rock wool curtains with asbestos cover on both sides, the lower by comparatively heavy roller curtains. The latter were, as experienced at Midway, a great hazard in bomb blast. In the *Unryū*s fire protection bulkheads (7 mm thick DS plates and also covered with asbestos) were used which closed horizontally by motor drive and manually in case of emergency. The guide in slots prevented the spread of gasoline into adjacent compartments. The locations were, as a rule, close to the elevators to isolate them from the hangar compartments. Branch pipes from the fire main were provided to spray bulkheads and curtains in an emergency."
8. The draft instructions stipulated that one-seat and two-seat planes were to be stored with unfolded wings, and only three-seat aircraft had to have folding wings. This may be the background to why only the torpedo bombers, such as "Kate," had folding wings, even though not as complete as aircraft of the USN.
9. There were connections for cooling water in the hangars, but this installation cannot be evaluated as useful firefighting equipment and was mainly for cooling down the fire protection bulkheads and curtains.
10. Only fighters were stowed in the forward portion of the upper hangar, which was supplied with ammunition by small hoists from the magazines.
11. The IJN did not use bombs heavier than 800 kg.
12. The warheads were stored in the magazines together with the torpedoes, while the exercise torpedoes were hung on the hangar walls.

Chapter 10

1. This stop was provided on the engine room side of all main steam lines passing through the boiler room bulkhead. It was a piston valve, which was held open when in use by the steam pressure under the seat but could be closed by the admission of steam to a piston. This operation could be controlled from the deck above.
2. Obviously done under battle conditions.